positioned for the
GIFTS

PREPARING ORDINARY PEOPLE FOR
EXTRAORDINARY POWER AND COMPASSION

Published by

Foursquare Missions Press

Positioned for the Gifts
Preparing Ordinary People for Extraordinary Power and Compassion
Stott/Hunt

ISBN: 978-0-578-54684-1

Editor: Laurie De Revere
Cover/Book Design: Wyce Ghiacy and Cheyne Jackson

Printed in the United States of America
1 2 3 4 5   22 21 20 19

Published by Foursquare Missions Press
4905 E. La Palma Ave.
Anaheim, CA 92807

Visit www.foursquaremissionspress.org

Acknowledgments

We are deeply appreciative to Laurie De Revere for her tireless and skilled editing of the manuscript. And to Wyce Ghiacy, an amazing graphic artist who designed, with Cheyne Jackson, our cover and did a terrific job laying out the book and internal graphics.

So grateful for the staff at Foursquare Missions Press (FMP) and their efforts to print this book. (All proceeds from the book will go to FMP and to ministry in the South Pacific.)

Finally, thank you to everyone who read the various versions of the manuscript and gave us invaluable input – we are in your debt.

Jerry and Bob

Dedication

To our incredible, beautiful, Spirit-filled wives.

Contents

What Others are Saying About
Positioned for the Gifts

Every so often a book comes along that captures the current move of the Spirit – *Positioned for the Gifts* is such a book! Biblically sound and story rich, it inspires every believer to be a vital part, using His gifts for His purposes in this generation.

I've encouraged the Church for many years to deepen its commitment to the "fellowship of His sufferings," but do so in the "power of His resurrection." *Positioned for the Gifts* blends both together, providing a practical roadmap for church and individual alike.

The stories will move you, the insights position you – allowing the Holy Spirit to fill you to touch a hurting world. This book is truly a "must read" for this generation!

Tommy Barnett
Global Pastor
Dream City Church, Phoenix
Los Angeles Dream Center, Los Angeles

I have been fast reading through your book!! What a treasure for today's church – worldwide! The gifts of the Spirit through this "instruction manual" are the power of heaven available for the church! The unity of the Spirit and the maturity of the saints, in Ephesians 4, comes about with the "tools" in operation to prepare the Bride. For the lost to be won we need the gift, as Jesus modeled with the woman at the well. The enemy's actions are discerned – the one who comes as an "angel of light," "seeking whom he may devour" with the gifts. An army of saints goes to spiritual "war" with the gifts, to see the kingdoms of this world become the Kingdoms of our Lord and our God. These are the weapons of heaven, the tools for harvest, and the adornment of the bride of Christ. He has come to Establish us, Equip us, Empower us, and Engage us, and all these take the operation of His gifts working through His children. Bob and Jerry have said it well, activated deeper hunger, and through heaven's inspiration, challenged us to be fully empowered to fulfill the purposes of God for our generation.

Carol Ward
Missionary, Founder/Director
Favor of God Ministry (Uganda, South Sudan)

Have you ever heard someone say, "The gifts of the Holy Spirit are not for today"? Dr. Jerry Stott and Bob Hunt did not receive that memo in time. Here they bring us a real world, modern day window into actual experiences with the Gifts of the Holy Spirit; but also train us in the solid theological underpinnings. These experiences and the teaching come from many cultures and contexts of the world. This is the kind of resource you will want, inspiring and yet grounding as well. It reminds me of Acts 1:1 referring to "all that Jesus began to *do and teach.*" This is a *doing and teaching* treasure that beckons us to adventure as we press into the Holy Spirit and the Gifts that are given to us.

Dr. Theodore Vail
Director of Foursquare Missions International

Pastor Jerry Stott is a practitioner when it comes to Spirit filled living and ministering in the power of the Holy Spirit. The fruitfulness of his ministry in healing, deliverance, miracles, church planting, and raising of disciples speaks for itself in Asia and the Pacific regions.

Here's another masterpiece from Jerry and Bob's heart to exhort, encourage, and equip the Church to minister in the fullness of the Holy Spirit.

The contents of this book would no doubt motivate and set the church ablaze for her forward march toward the end time harvest.

Leslie Keegel (D.Min, D.D)
Chairman Foursquare Global Council
President Foursquare Church
Sri Lanka

Any Bible academic can attempt to explain "the gifts of the Spirit," but only Spirit-empowered veterans like Dr. Jerry Stott and Bob Hunt can unveil their true meanings using powerful and real-life stories. As you read through this book, your eyes will be opened to how the gifts of the Spirit are both absolutely necessary and absolutely available to reach the world for Christ. You will be moved to tears as the mysteries of the supernatural become clear and as the Holy Spirit beckons your partnership. May what you read on these pages become your new way of life!

Jerry Dirmann
Senior Pastor, The Rock, Anaheim, CA

I once heard the late John Wimber, founder of the Vineyard Movement of churches, share his testimony of conversion and ministry beginnings. As a new believer, he immersed himself in the scriptures and came to the conclusion that the New Testament lifestyle was to be one of supernatural enablement and ministry. Therefore, he approached his pastor and asked a simple question, "When do we get to do the stuff?"

I wonder if our churches aren't filled with people asking the same question? An honest reading of the New Testament would lead one to the obvious conclusion that Jesus is offering us a supernatural life that begins upon conversion and extends into the age to come.

Jerry Stott and Bob Hunt's book, *Positioned for the Gifts: Preparing Ordinary People for Extraordinary Power and Compassion* is a much-needed resource that not only embraces this call to a dynamic life of spirit-empowered ministry, but also serves to equip and empower the believer for such a call. The content is not only biblically sourced; it is also practically illustrated through the miraculous ministry of Jerry and Bob's own life and experience. I believe the message of this book is needed more than ever.

Randy Remington
Senior Pastor, Beaverton Foursquare Church
President-Elect, The Foursquare Church

Jerry and Bob share a time when the Holy Spirit spoke loud and clear; "That's my Church. But they have forgotten their assignment. They are enjoying the fellowship. They are enjoying my Word. They are enjoying my blessings. But they forgot their assignment—go into all the world and preach the gospel...His last word, 'Go'...Jesus has given us authority...*And these signs will follow those who believe.* Mark 16:17"

May the Holy Spirit use this book and Jerry and Bob's personal experiences to awaken the Church to our shared mission as well as a hunger to receive power to be His witnesses with all the signs following!

Dr. Jim Scott
Associate Director, Foursquare Missions International

For over a decade now I consider Jerry Stott one of my closest friends. And in the years that the Lord has given me the privilege to know Jerry, I really have not come across many people who possess the integrity and giftedness along with an incorruptible heart like Jerry Stott.

In this book, *Positioned For The Gifts*, Jerry and Bob Hunt lay out a mission, a mandate, and a mechanism for the gifts to bless God's people, through the empowering of the Holy Spirit. I am convinced that this book will equip and inspire you and that there are many more books to come!

Mike Kai
Inspire Church Network, Senior Pastor
Author of The Pound For Pound Principle and Plateaus

After seeing Jerry minister at our church, and interviewing him on the radio, I know he doesn't just talk about the gifts of the Spirit, he functions in the gifts of the Spirit. This book is a timely reminder to the Body of Christ that we need to "Eagerly desire Spiritual Gifts." One of the great things about Jerry's perspective is that he's ministered in many different nations and has seen the same biblical principles in action all over the world. I believe many people will be equipped and released to function in the Spiritual Gifts as a result of this book.

Pastor Matt Prater
New Hope Church Brisbane, Historymakers Radio

In this book, *Positioned for the Gifts,* you will be encouraged to take the admonition of the apostle Paul to his young student, Timothy, "to stir up the gift of God which is in you through the laying on of my hands. For God has not given us a spirit of fear, but of power and of love and of a sound mind." 2 Timothy 1:6-7. The authors suggest that the gifts of God within believers have been given for specific reasons. One of those reasons is to aid us in doing the Father's business, which is seeking and bringing to salvation those that are lost.

The gifts of God are not for ownership. They are the gifts of the Holy Spirit to flow through the lives of believers to empower them to minister to others. The needs people have exist everywhere, not just in a church service.

Be encouraged by this book to allow the Holy Spirit to use you in ministry to those you encounter day by day. Also, as spirit-filled, Pentecostal believers, we should continue to yield to the Holy Spirit in our church services so that those gathered will be blessed and encouraged, healed and delivered by the power of God.

Dr. Sterling Brackett
Former LIFE East President,
Chief Operating Officer (retired) The Foursquare Church

...I see the last day revival that's going to usher in the precious fruit of the earth. It will be the greatest revival the world has ever seen! It's going to be a wave of the gifts of the Spirit. The ministry gifts will be flowing on this planet earth.

— Portion of a prophetic word given to Lester Sumrall
by Smith Wigglesworth in 1939

positioned for the

GIFTS

PREPARING ORDINARY PEOPLE FOR
EXTRAORDINARY POWER AND COMPASSION

STOTT/HUNT

Introduction

This is a book about the nine gifts of the Holy Spirit, offered to everyday believers in Jesus Christ, listed in 1 Corinthians chapter 12.

It's written, both with real life stories and biblical truth, to encourage average people to step out in faith and make the supernatural a natural part of life.

It's a journey both authors have taken and continue to take. This book is as much for them as for anyone reading it. Moving in the power of the Holy Spirit is not something you can bottle and store. Like manna from heaven, it needs to be fresh everyday.

In some ways the words you are about to read could be described as a battlefield strategy handbook. The Gifts are meant for battle, Kingdom of God warfare. Yes, they are intended to encourage the Body of Christ, but they also take ground from the enemy of our souls. And this ground is not easily seized.

The authors write fully aware of a current prophetic stream, coursing globally, of a coming Holy Spirit empowerment to those who desire to serve the purposes of God for their generation. Throughout the writing there was a deep sense that this new, younger generation would be the one that would take Kingdom warfare to the next level. (Yet, their hope is that the book will be as meaningful to the 80-year-old warrior as it is to the 18-year-old.)

To the pastor, the leader who both wants to grow in the Gifts and to see others come along, the authors write as former pastors who are fiercely committed to the local church. The Church was, at the time Paul wrote, and still is today, the community to risk and learn, and then to go and do. Their prayer is that this book will be a resource, a road map for your congregation to experience the joy of supernatural living.

The authors know that in using a term like "Kingdom Warrior" it may seem exclusionary to those who love the Lord but wonder where they fit in such a spiritual battle. Maybe you are raising children and, frankly, that is all "the battle" you can handle. That's real. Moving in the gifts of the Spirit, however, can and should be something experienced in the home. Our spiritual lives are lived more there than anywhere else. And what could be more authentic, more formative, than our children seeing us move in the spiritual realm as naturally as we do in the physical world?

So, who are the "ordinary people" referred to in the subtitle? We live in a culture that worships those who receive the most attention – through TV, radio, internet... even the pulpit. No disrespect to those who have the spotlight of media upon them, but most of us do not. We may live outside the limelight, but the brightest light of our Lord shines on us as we encounter everyday life. This book is for the rest of us who want all the Lord has for us – nothing more, but nothing less. Everyday life may be the most exciting adventure of all.

You'll soon note that the authors wrote as one voice, sharing stories without individual attribution, for the sake of rhythm and flow throughout.

Finally, the authors wish to encourage you to pray and to ask the Holy Spirit to lead you throughout the reading of this book. The gifts of the Spirit cannot be fully comprehended apart from the Spirit of God. And, prayer is so critical if we are not only to understand, but also to apply what we have read.

May the Spirit of the Lord guide us into all truth. (John 16:13)

Chapter One

The New Kingdom Warrior

I knew the voice inside me. It would come quietly, speak softly, and then leave with its words repeating in my memory. This time it came with an emotion, one that I was not accustomed to, like the feeling that accompanies a stern warning from your father. The message came clear, direct, and with force.

Leave quickly.

The team of a dozen mainly college age students that I had been leading by boat up and down the various tributaries of the Amazon River in Brazil were now expecting the supernatural. Blind eyes gaining full sight and deaf ears recovering total hearing bookended a wide spectrum of healing of mostly the "Riberenos," or river people. Rare was the person who walked away not touched by God. I had seen healing before, but not of this magnitude and consistency. Word was getting out that God was with us.

One more adventure awaited my team as they stayed in the boat on the shore below, a white sandy knoll where I and my interpreter met the leader of this village, an older man, shirtless, wearing tattered tan shorts and cheap plastic sandals. Usually within moments serious faces gave way to smiles. The people were hospitable to a fault, especially to a boat full of Americans who had "brought their God."

This time was different. No smiles or giggling laughter greeted us. At the same time, the voice came. Without changing my rather forced smile, I spoke to the interpreter, "Let's go." She seemed puzzled both at their responses and at my reply – but even more so when I told her, "Don't take your eyes off of them. Keep smiling, and let's back up slowly to the boat." With our faces toward the strangers, but our legs moving in the opposite direction, we stumbled down the sandy embankment, reaching the boat.

"Everybody stay inside. Let's shove off!" As soon as we turned our backs on the river people, the rocks, partially hidden by the twilight, began to whirl passed our heads and hit the metal boat – big rocks from everywhere, slamming against the roof of the boat as if the jungle itself had come alive with rage. Beginning our unplanned retreat, we marveled that no one was struck – a miracle in and of itself.

Whether the Holy Spirit graced me at that moment with a word of wisdom, word of knowledge, or both, I'm not sure. But without question, the voice inside didn't originate with me – it came from God. I and my team, however, were fortunate beneficiaries because I knew how to listen.

The Powerful Purposed Life

Listen to the voice of the Spirit. Move in the gifts of the Spirit. Be a believer who is able and willing to use every divine resource available to achieve the purposes of God for this generation. And, do it all with love – this is the new Kingdom Warrior.

Dynamic young author A.J. Swoboda succinctly and simply said to a group of 4,000 of his peers:

"When you walk in the Spirit, you see things differently."[1]

There is a growing group, comprised across generational and ethnic lines, that gets it; the day of the exalted, single personality driven ministry is passing and is giving way to an army of average, everyday individuals. These are believers who are hungry for God, solid in the Word, and steeped in the primacy of love. Their humility makes them keenly aware that they cannot gain ground in hand-to-hand Kingdom warfare – unless their weapons are of the Spirit.

Their faith is not merely some quaint, personal expression or a parental or cultural appendage – it is tied to something much larger and beyond themselves. They are the new cloud of witnesses, sharing a common passion passed down for over two thousand years. They are the warriors who fight to establish the Kingdom of God.

> *For we are his workmanship, created in Christ Jesus for good works, which God prepared beforehand, that we should walk in them.* Ephesians 2:10

> *For the weapons of our warfare are not carnal, but mighty through God to the pulling down of strongholds.* 2 Corinthians 10:4

The late professor from Dallas Theological Seminary, Merrill F. Unger, understood this years ago:

"But the Christian warrior, steadfastly refusing to surrender the ground which is his in Christ and availing himself of the full armor of God, maintains his Spirit-filled experience. He is therefore invincible. The power of God in his life, as he is thus protected through satanic temptation and attack, now becomes available for an effectual ministry, bringing blessing to men and glory to God."[2]

Apostolic leader from Cambodia, Ted Olbrich, missionary and leader of one of the fastest church planting movements in the world, recently wrote on Facebook about the fearlessness and focus needed in today's leaders:

> "Prayers for the sick result in healings and a church is born. It really isn't rocket science, say I. There are two things that paralyze most churches: They give lip service to the Holy Spirit but don't totally depend on His leadership and power, so nothing happens. Or, they are so hung up on their own failures, imperfections and sin they are convinced God won't use them. So He doesn't. Everywhere I go I do everything I can to cast down both lies. The Holy Spirit is alive and well, and is powerful as ever, you just have to believe in it. So confess, repent, and get over yourselves! Believe in His desire to use YOU and then have the guts to act like it. That'll do."[3]

The world does not need cool Christians who are culturally saturated. It needs exiles with the scent of heaven and the aroma of Christ.

This new warrior, of whom age is irrelevant, cares more about Kingdom than the surrounding, encroaching culture. The world has lost its grip on these servants of God. In the eloquent words of John Piper:

"The world does not need cool Christians who are culturally saturated. It needs exiles with the scent of heaven and the aroma of Christ."[4]

This new warrior understands the boundaries of this Kingdom of God, the "already but not yet."[5] They live in the realities of the fullness of the Spirit while being buffeted by the enemy and the flesh. They are realists based in the ideals of Scripture.

Paul wrote the following in a vulnerable time in his life:

> *Therefore, since through God's mercy we have this ministry, we do not lose heart. Rather, we have renounced secret and shameful ways; we do not use deception, nor do we distort the word of God...The god of this age has blinded the minds of unbelievers, so that they cannot see the light of the gospel...* 2 Corinthians 4:1-4

> *But we have this treasure in jars of clay to show that this all-surpassing power is from God and not from us. We are hard pressed on every side, but not crushed; perplexed, but not in despair; persecuted, but not abandoned; struck down, but not destroyed.* 2 Corinthians 4:7-9

This new warrior seeks to be authentic, because Jesus was and is authentic. This drives them to be the same person raising their hands in church to worship as they are in the classroom raising their hand to ask a question – or, that their voice of praise to God be the same voice of love to their neighbor. It also drives them to reject the ordinary and to push the boundaries of faith.

"Life is too short, the world is too big and God's love is too great to live ordinary."[6] Christine Caine

This new warrior has battled sin and has found freedom in grace. They know the toll on the human condition of missing the mark and how to extend God's tender mercies. They will walk in the fruit of the Spirit hand in hand with those crushed in spirit.

In the words of writer Tullian Tchividjian:

"Churches that will thrive in any meaningful way going forward, will not be castles of purity… but rather basements of grace where broken sinners are embraced and forgiven; places where sin doesn't shock and grace still amazes."[7]

This new warrior knows to ask the Spirit to gift them to go, to serve the purposes of God for their generation. Many of these purposes lie outside the confines of Sunday morning and the walls of the church. They are driven by the Spirit to take their message to the marketplace.

One of the early warriors in the Spirit, Dr. Jerry Cook, said it well:

> "The gifts of the Spirit, as I understand them, are God's means of getting to people and meeting their needs through believers. I do not believe the spiritual gifts were meant primarily for the sanctuary. Some of them can operate there, and that's fine, but many of them were primarily designed for the street."[8]

The clash of kingdoms is accelerating; old wineskins will not work.

A Prophetic Move

Many older leaders, Kingdom warriors themselves, sense the move of the Spirit to release believers outside the comfort of the Church and into a chaotic world. Because they will be armed with power and established in love with a heart for the lost, they will be the generation that shakes the Church out of any fear and apathy. The clash of kingdoms is accelerating; old wineskins will not work.

Clint Pickrel is a respected leader, rancher, entrepreneur, and retired pastor. The Lord has burdened his heart with the following message:

"Some years ago the Lord spoke to my heart and said, 'You're a part of a David Generation.'

"David was known as a man of war. Most of my peers, men and women, have fought many battles. We've sacrificed, paid a price, costing us in ways we've never gotten back. But we didn't do it for ourselves – we did it for the next generation.

"David's accomplishment wasn't just to establish Israel as a national force, but to establish Solomon as king – with nearly unlimited resources, no need for continued fighting and bloodshed – so that his son could build the temple of God. (To establish the Kingdom of God for his generation.)

"Solomon didn't look or act like David. He carried forth a legacy that established Israel as a political force, but he also built the temple that brought forth the presence of Almighty God.

"There is a Solomon Generation that God is raising up that is given the task to establish the presence of God like we have never seen, possibly in the history of the world.

"In our generation, much of the move of the Spirit was very church-centered, even though we reached the world and focused on the lost. But, so much of where the gifts of the Spirit moved was in our church service.

"The Solomon Generation will not look like that. The Solomon Generation is a move of God in the marketplace. It's not going to be church-centric – not that the church will be less important, but it will send a generation outside its walls and into the streets.

"The Solomon Generation will be every bit as Spirit-filled, Spirit-empowered, moving in the might of the Gifts, but they will do it beyond Sunday morning to reach the lost. Word of knowledge, prophecy, working of miracles, healing will happen in the marketplace.

"This Solomon Generation will establish the presence of God in a supernatural manner that we, the David Generation, hungered for, we fasted for, we cried for, we fought for. And the manifestation of our dream is in front of us.

"This season is so significant because we are resourcing a younger generation that will not look like us, talk like us, sound like us. But they are going to do as much as we've ever dreamed of and more. This is the juncture of history we are in. We are impacting the next 50 years. This Solomon Generation could very well be the generation that ushers in the Second Coming of Christ."[9]

No more time for theological squabbles or waiting. It's time to do, to go, and to be armed and ready. This book is dedicated to challenging all of us toward that end. Its focus is on the nine gifts enumerated in 1 Corinthians 12 for the purpose of winning the world, in the same way Jesus did. This is not a theological treatise, rather a combination of personal stories and a biblical understanding of the Gifts.

Hopefully, prayerfully, it is a book full of spiritual truth and inspiration that causes you to hunger for Kingdom warfare and Kingdom blessing – to serve His purposes.

Now concerning spiritual gifts, brethren, I do not want you to be ignorant: You know that you were Gentiles, carried away to these dumb idols, however you were led. Therefore I make known to you that no one speaking by the Spirit of God calls Jesus accursed, and no one can say that Jesus is Lord except by the Holy Spirit.

There are diversities of gifts, but the same Spirit. There are differences of ministries, but the same Lord. And there are diversities of activities, but it is the same God who works all in all. But the manifestation of the Spirit is given to each one for the profit of all: for to one is given the word of wisdom through the Spirit, to another the word of knowledge through the same Spirit, to another faith by the same Spirit, to another gifts of healings by the same Spirit, to another the working of miracles, to another prophecy, to another discerning of spirits, to another different kinds of tongues, to another the interpretation of tongues. But one and the same Spirit works all these things, distributing to each one individually as He wills. **1 Corinthians 12:1-11**

Chapter Two

The Gifts are for You!

Walking toward the medical clinic, as the sun rose over the gray hills in Cap-Haitien, Haiti, I saw the line of people, quiet and dignified, waiting. Closer, I began to see only mothers, or grandmothers holding babies in their arms or young children by the hand.

The line stretched for at least a half-mile. Arriving at the clinic, on my first day of service, I rather naively asked, "How can I help?"

"We need you in triage." Her curt reply left me baffled. To myself I said, "What is triage?" Without asking that question, the nurse, an obvious veteran of the clinic, gave me simple yet terrifying instructions. "You will choose which ones see the doctor. We can't see them all. Pick the ones that look the sickest and tell the others to come back next week."

Before I could protest that I had neither the medical background nor the language skills to choose which babies and children would get help that day, she abruptly left. As the rush of mothers pleading to me in their native Creole, with sick babies crying, pinned me into a corner, the thought stabbed me – I may be choosing which ones would live and which ones would die. But I had no time for self-pity or introspection.

In that moment, I asked God for wisdom and for the Holy Spirit's gift of wisdom – I had no one or no where else to turn. I believe He helped me choose wisely that day.

The Right Stuff

The camouflaged hunter drew closer to his prey. Placing his body and bow in position, he reached back to the quiver for one of his finely honed arrows. His fingers searched for an arrow, any arrow, but none were found and his prize was lost.

No bow hunter would leave for the hunt without arrows. No farmer would till the fields without a proper plow. To analogize for the young urban culture: No millennial would have a smart phone without apps.

Any time you go to battle without your weapons properly functioning you cannot expect to win the fight.

We all need the right tools to accomplish a task and to fulfill a mission. So, two questions for every believer: *Are you currently and properly equipped to serve the purposes of God for this generation?* And, more specifically, *Are you living your spiritual life operating with or without the spiritual gifts?* God gives them to us for a distinct mission or for a specific purpose. So, a third question must be asked: *Why are so many afraid, ignorant, or unwilling to use the Gifts outlined in 1 Corinthians 12?*

Old Pentecostal warrior, the late Lester Sumrall, states it bluntly:

> "The church today is going into battle without a true knowledge of those weapons. Any time you go to battle without your weapons properly functioning you cannot expect to win the fight."[1]

New warrior, Christine Caine, says it humorously in terms of our utter need to depend on the Holy Spirit as a fundamental starting point:

> "People ask me if you need the Holy Ghost to go to Heaven. Honey, you need the Holy Ghost to go to Walmart."[2]

You Talkin' to Me?

Spiritual gifts – how do they work? What are they and what are their purposes? Why do so few Christians seem to move in them? How can I move in them? Do I need to be more spiritual? Are the spiritual gifts really for me?

To answer the last question first, I can't say it enough: <u>The spiritual gifts are for you!</u>

The problem is, however, few are asking the questions and fewer pulpits are telling the story. People simply don't know what they could have. And the Church suffers; even worse, the world misses out on a power, not of this world, that proclaims the gospel to the poor, the captives, the blind, and the oppressed (Luke 4:18).

The late John Wimber lamented often that the problem with the Body of Christ is that they don't ask the question, "Lord, what are you doing?" And they don't make themselves available to hear what He is doing and then act.

I remember a television show that highlighted a group of millionaires. These millionaires shared one thing in common – they all started with nothing. At the end of the show, the interviewer asked them all a question, "Now, what would you do if you lost all your money?"

Each one in their own way said the same thing, "Well, I could make it all back again."

The incredulous interviewer asked, "How can you be so sure?"

One millionaire offered a reply, "I could make all my money back in three years."

The host challenged his bold guest, "Really? And how do you know that?"

The success-from-scratch individual offered a classic answer, "Because, I know something you don't know."

The Apostle Paul, in 1 Corinthians 12, is basically telling the church in Corinth the same thing, "Concerning the spiritual gifts, I don't want you to be ignorant. I want to tell you something you don't know." And, at least the church Paul addressed moved in the Gifts! The level of understanding in some churches today regarding these Gifts is tragic.

Tragic because once a believer and a community of believers begin to move in the power of the Spirit and operate in His Gifts, they begin to experience first hand the joy the disciples knew when Jesus first sent them out, two by two. After driving out many demons and healing many sick people, they returned with joy. Who wouldn't? I've led dozens of short-term teams around the world, almost always with similar results as those first disciples; and every time, team members come back changed forever. Why? They experienced the compassionate power of God.

Jesus, after rejoicing in the Spirit and speaking to the 70, turned privately to his twelve:

> Instead of the Gifts being a normal, expected expression of the healthy church, we often treat them like the unexpected and uninvited guest to our home.

> *Blessed are the eyes which see the things you see; for I tell you that many prophets and kings have desired to see what you see, and have not seen it, and to hear what you hear, and have not heard it."* **Luke 10:23-24**

The Naturalness of the Supernatural

Instead of the Gifts being a normal, expected expression of the healthy church, we often treat them like the unexpected and uninvited guest to our home. We may invite them in, but we aren't sure what to do; and we hope they don't stay too long.

The late, great Jerry Cook said it best, of course:

"We call in experts from all over the country to teach about the Holy Spirit. This communicates to our people how difficult it is to be filled in the Holy Spirit. We hire evangelists from all over the world to come and conduct healing campaigns. This communicates that only an expert can minister healing. We have seminars and conferences on every conceivable subject. They can be helpful, I suppose, but too often we are communicating that living supernaturally in a natural way is technical and difficult.

"Any believer filled with the Spirit has the supernatural power of Jesus to meet any situation and put any demonic power to flight. The name of Jesus is powerful in the mouth of a believer. It's not more powerful in one person's mouth than it is in the mouth of any other believer. We make specialties out of ministry. We make Christian service difficult. Ministry is the natural flow of Jesus' life through us even when we may not be aware of it."[3]

"Would he touch me too?" she cried out, like a scene from the New Testament. The tiny woman in old clothes would eventually be one of the first healings in our church, coming after a serious time dedicated to prayer and believing God for the miraculous.

Our church's citywide food and clothing distribution center thrived, and people always lined up early to be the first to receive. The city warned us that we could not force people to go to our church in order to receive food or any other items from the ministry. Forcing anyone to do anything never works.

Since we had a large staff that gathered early to set up and prepare for distribution, I figured no one could stop me from having a service with my own church workers. So, while people were getting in early to be first in line to receive, I would have a time of praise and worship with our staff, and conveniently, a short sermon for them, which the recipients had to listen to before the distribution began.

That particular Saturday I was speaking from Luke 8:43-48:

And a woman who had a hemorrhage for twelve years, and could not be healed by anyone, came up behind Him and touched the fringe of His cloak, and immediately her hemorrhage stopped. And Jesus said, "Who is the one who touched Me?" And while they were all denying it, Peter said, "Master, the people are crowding and pressing in on You." But Jesus said, "Someone did touch Me, for I was aware that power had gone out of Me." When the woman saw that she had not escaped notice, she came trembling and fell down before Him, and declared in the presence of all the people the reason why she had touched Him, and how she had been immediately healed. And He said to her, "Daughter, your faith has made you well; go in peace."

All of a sudden, a woman who was waiting in line shouted out, "Would he touch me too?" Shocked by her boldness, I immediately invited her up for prayer. She was disabled and could not walk on one leg. I asked our staff to join with me in prayer for this broken, but faith-filled, woman. As soon as we laid hands on her, the bad leg became completely normal, allowing her to walk around in joy. The staff, and even those waiting, began praising God.

This was the first breakthrough in our church before a wave of the miraculous crashed over us. Within just weeks of that healing, we began to see the blind healed and even those born deaf, hearing. And it all happened so naturally.

The Need for the Anointing

The Spirit of the Lord is upon Me, because He has anointed Me to preach the gospel to the poor; He has sent Me to heal the brokenhearted, to proclaim liberty to the captives and recovery of sight to the blind, to set at liberty those who are oppressed. Luke 4:18

It shall come to pass in that day that his burden will be taken away from your shoulder, and his yoke from your neck, and the yoke will be destroyed because of the anointing oil. Isaiah 10:27

The fuel, the power for Kingdom building, is the anointing. The anointing is that thing which is needed to break through the kingdom of darkness. Yet the anointing is "not an impartation of something, but someone."[4]

And, the person moving in the anointing of the Holy Spirit will know the gifts of the Holy Spirit.

Bill Johnson correctly states:

"This anointing is actually the person of the Holy Spirit upon someone to equip them for supernatural endeavors."[5]

To truly take ground for the Kingdom of God, to advance His church, to preach the gospel, an anointing must flow. And, the person moving in the anointing of the Holy Spirit will know the gifts of the Holy Spirit. They will flow out as a natural part of life.

We desperately need a movement of people that are anointed. Anointed people rarely seek title or position. Anointed believers "seek first the Kingdom of God" because they have "tasted and seen that the Lord is good." (Psalm 34:8) Anointed believers know God with their mind and their heart and their soul. They've experienced the presence of God, and nothing else in their world compares.

Being anointed, moving in the Gifts, is not an "on and off" button, but rather a lifestyle of living in his presence.

Anointed ones also know the power in death to self.

"I have been crucified with Christ; it is no longer I who live but Christ lives in me..." Galatians 2:20

They know the anointing oil flows from a submission to the Spirit, "Not my will, but yours." (Luke 22:42)

Being anointed, moving in the Gifts, is not an "on and off" button, but rather a lifestyle of living in his presence.

Dr. Leslie Keegel says it well:

"If there is a real anointing, it flows from a deep understanding of the Holy Spirit based in a lifestyle committed to the Triune God."[6]

Dr. Keegel's ultimate vision is to see leaders across the globe relying "completely on the anointing of the Holy Spirit to preach the message of the Good News..."[7]

This Good News must extend, Dr. Keegel notes, to the poor, sick, discouraged, depressed, and disenfranchised. It must also include a prophetic message of Jesus' return.[8]

The anointing of the Lord is available to anyone and everyone. Intellectual capacity and charismatic personality do not inhibit or enhance the anointing. In fact, those that society deems least significant, with the anointing of God, can break yokes that the most gifted cannot. God often uses the weak to confound the wise. (1 Corinthians 1:27)

A story by Dr. Tony Campolo, told years ago when I was a junior high youth pastor, literally kept me in the ministry. I often, jokingly, tell anyone wanting to be in full-time ministry that they should begin with junior-highers (ages 12, 13, 14). If you can minister to them, at an age that defies humanity, you can minister to anyone. Tony shared how he spoke at a junior high camp up in the mountains. As with most youth camps, there was a "talent" night when individual kids show off skills or talents ranging from the gifted to the absurd. In this particular camp, each cabin chose someone to represent them in front of the entire camp. One of the boys' cabins thought it would be "funny" to have a junior-higher with severe cerebral palsy to be their selection.

When the big night came, various junior campers performed in front of a typically raucous young crowd. When this disabled young boy began to walk on the

God's presence is discovered in repentance.

stage, the room filled with a muffled laughter. He literally had to drag his neurologically impaired body to the podium. The laughter got louder until he spoke with contorted facial muscles and the staccato stuttering of words.

"Jeee-sus." Those two syllables seemed to take forever. "Loves me." That short phrase flowed more easily. But the last phrase did not. "And I love Jesus."

As Campolo tells the story, and I still remember it vividly, there was dead silence. Soon the laughter turned to weeping. Repentance broke out among the young hearts in the large hall.

"God's presence is discovered in repentance."[9]

From that camp experience, many junior-highers not only encountered the risen Christ, but went on to become ministers of the gospel.

The Kingdom warrior will not always be the most beautiful, talented, or intelligent. They will, however, be the kind of servant willing to be mocked, just as Jesus was mocked.

Anointing Vs. Gifting

There is a video that has gone viral of Christine Caine, Australian speaker extraordinaire, on the topic of the anointing of God. I've watched it several times. In her message she makes the critical distinction between gifting and anointing. In this instance she is not referring to the gifting of the Spirit, but natural gifting, such as persuasive speaking.

> "Gifting and anointing are two different things. A gifting can fill a room, a gifting entertains, a gifting wows people. But the Bible doesn't say a gifting breaks the yoke and chain – it says the anointing breaks the yoke and chain."

There is a tendency for the church to elevate, to their young leaders, those deemed as gifted, even to the point of wanting a certain look – the more attractive the better.

Giftedness can often take priority over character and spiritual maturity. The anointing gets lost in the drive to raise up gifted, beautiful and driven people.

> "So we don't need more gifted ministers."

Christine Caine continues:

> "We need a whole lot more anointed people that are willing to go through the crushing so that there is an oil."

As stated before, the anointing often comes with a price – your life laid down at the foot of the King. It's from the hard struggle to transfer your will for His will that anointing comes.

What I most love about her video is the end purpose of the anointing – a "supernaturally natural" flow of His love to others.

"So when people come to you at your workplace, to your home, over dinner, when you're at the supermarket talking to that girl at the checkout, the anointing will break the yokes and chains and the bondages."

Anointed, ordinary people, flowing in the gifts of the Spirit, can take back territory for the King and His Kingdom.

It's the heart of this book: ordinary people (often in ordinary situations) moving in extraordinary power.

"We need anointed people for the Kingdom of God."[10]

Amen!

Anointed, ordinary people, flowing in the gifts of the Spirit, can take back territory for the King and His Kingdom.

Where We Need to Go

> "The goal of the Kingdom is to make things as they should be – a work in progress until God brings all things to its completion. We partner with God in the advancement of his kingdom through proclaiming and living Kingdom shaped lives in the present age, praying for it to be 'on earth as it is in heaven.'"[11]

On the other end of the evangelical, theological spectrum from Ed Stetzer, Bill Johnson asks a question that looms whenever we discuss the Kingdom of God:

> "This leaves us with a question that has yet to be answered; What generation will host Him until the Kingdom of the world becomes the Kingdom of our Lord and Christ? (See Revelation 11:15)"[12]

The evangelical church is experiencing the Kingdom of the *already but not yet* in differing ways, but with a very similar purpose.

Let's have a little fun…

Imagine an elevator that could take various portions of the evangelical church to the floor that would allow them to experience, in fullness, the Kingdom of God…

Charismatic/Pentecostal churches missed their floor because they pushed all the buttons in the elevator.

Social justice churches missed their floor because they were too busy cleaning out the elevator.

Attractional churches missed their floor because they were just so happy to fill the elevator.

Missional churches missed their floor because they decided to involve everyone by taking the stairs.

And the Baptists? (Because the Baptists deserve their own section…) After they missed their floor, they simply bought the building.

We are all, hopefully, moving toward the same destination; how we get there, what methods we employ, will differ.

But we most definitely should learn from each other so we don't miss the floor!

Getting Off on the Right Floor

> *The Kingdom of God is near. Repent and believe the good news!* Mark 1:15

Theologian N.T. Wright in regards to the Kingdom states: "God's future was breaking into the present. Heaven was arriving on earth"[13]

The focus of Jesus' ministry – the Kingdom of God being established "on earth as it is in heaven" – would look very different than the kingdom His fellow Jews envisioned at the time. It would take more than rhetoric to change their minds, let alone their hearts.

It would take a miracle... miracles, in fact. John Wimber has stated:

> "Every miraculous act had a purpose: to confront people with His message that in Him the Kingdom of God had come and that they had to decide to accept or reject it."[14]

While we can, and must, learn from our brothers and sisters from various traditions, both old and new, our ultimate model to advancing the Kingdom comes from Jesus and the men He discipled. And, if a generation living now will be hosting His arrival, even more the need to position ourselves to move in the same power and giftings of two thousand years ago.

The Kingdom of God must be advanced. How we do so will vary from movements, local churches, and even individuals.

But, we all can use the same tools, and the Holy Spirit is offering them to all.

Jesus wants to bless us once again so that we might be a blessing. Besides the lack of teaching on the Gifts in many of today's churches, there are a few reasons that stop this incredible blessing. There are real challenges that "keep us in the elevator," never experiencing the fullness of Kingdom life and the use of His Gifts.

• Pride/Peer Pressure

If sins could be labeled by how bad they are, pride would inevitably be at the top. There are different kinds of pride, but the pride of Proverbs 8:13 and Psalm 10:4 is rooted in self-righteousness; and God hates it. Why? Because, it is a huge hindrance to seeking Him. God wants nothing to come between you and Him. Tim Keller calls pride the "carbon monoxide of sin. It silently and slowly kills you without you even knowing." Pride can also imperceptibly keep you from the Gifts.

"The Gifts seem weird." Translation: They are not acceptable or "cool" in a society dominated by peer pressure created in large part by Hollywood, Hip Hop, and Silicon Valley. But, we believers were told by Jesus himself that we'd be persecuted for our beliefs. Operating on a supernatural level means that which is not natural or operating according to the laws of nature. So, yes, moving in the Gifts should seem different. "Weird" is an ambiguous, arbitrary, biased term that became a catchall to things we don't understand or don't want to understand.

But God has chosen the foolish (weird) *things of the world to put to shame the wise.* 1 Corinthians 1:27

"What would others think?" is usually a question rooted in pride. In a world full of peer pressure, which is real, it takes courage to follow up that question with, "But, what would God think?" Fear of Man vs. Fear of God – as old as Adam and Eve. It is a battle we all face at times.

If fear of man dominates your heart and mind, the spiritual gifts will seem like obstacles to be overcome in your quest for acceptance.

Under which domain will we ultimately operate? If fear of man dominates your heart and mind, the spiritual gifts will seem like obstacles to be overcome in your quest for acceptance.

Smith Wigglesworth, someone who was never associated with the fear of man, wrote these colorful, yet insightful words:

"Pentecost came with the sound of a mighty, rushing wind, a violent blast from heaven! Heaven has not exhausted its blasts, but our danger is we are getting frightened of them."[15]

- **Ignorance**

> *Now concerning spiritual gifts, brethren, I do not want you to be ignorant.* 1 Corinthians 12:1

Paul, in writing his letter to the church in Corinth, was well aware of the many problems this church faced. Part of the solution was to operate in the Gifts in a healthy manner. Lack of knowledge, especially on spiritual issues, is never a good thing.

Ignorance regarding the spiritual gifts has plagued the Church, from Corinth to today. There are many sincere believers who believe the Gifts were only for the Apostles and the first church – that they are no longer needed today. However, my guess is that most of the believers who do not operate in the Gifts are either unaware of their existence or believe they are for somebody else.

To quote Dr. Craig Keener:

"Most of the global church recognizes that the God who poured out the Spirit on the day of Pentecost did not pour the Spirit back afterwards!"[16]

Amen. What the so called "third world" or "developing nations" church lacks in formal theological training, they more than make up by moving in the power of the Holy Spirit.

- **Fear**

> *Therefore I remind you to stir up the gift of God which is in you through the laying on of my hands. For God has not given us a spirit of fear, but of power and of love and of a sound mind.* 2 Timothy 1:6-7

Paul needed to challenge young Timothy to keep moving in the Gifts (*charismata*) and to not let fear stop him. Again, some things haven't changed in 2,000 years – fear can strip us of God's most important tools. And we are not the only ones that are affected negatively, but also those God wants us to reach.

Fear often finds roots in the unknown. What we don't know can scare us. One of the greatest challenges facing the believer today is the fear of what might occur if one should fully relinquish control of their life and mind and emotions to the Holy Spirit.

According to global teacher, Dr. Daniel Brown:

"Many believers unknowingly opt out of their rightful inheritance and dismiss a miraculous grace-gift from the Lord because they do not want to experience anything supernatural – like being able to pray in a language their mind never learned or being alerted to facts and understanding their mind could never know on its own." [17]

I've noticed that believers' fear is often rooted in over-mystifying the process of moving in the Gifts. It all seems too ethereal, "out there" – one big mystery of God. I agree with Mike Bickle of the International House of Prayer (IHOP) who has insightfully stated:

> Moving in the Gifts is not comfortable. No matter how many times you move in them, there is always a step of faith.

"In order to grow in the prophetic or in being used by the Holy Spirit and the gifts of the Holy Spirit we need to demystify the process in our understanding."[18]

I'm not sure if Mike coined the phrase "supernaturally natural," but he artfully uses it to describe his contention that there is both a spiritual side and a human, natural side in moving in the Spirit. We'll explore this in more depth in Chapter 12.

• Comfortability

In an age where hard work seems like a threat to society, for many, being comfortable is the highest of unspoken priorities. Moving in the Gifts is not comfortable. No matter how many times you move in them, there is always a step of faith. Faith, when activated, isn't comfortable. John Wimber once said that faith is spelled R-I-S-K. You can't take ground for the Kingdom from the comfort of the couch. Jesus said the most uncomfortable of statements:

> *If the world hates you, you know that it hated Me before it hated you.* John 15:18

It's never comfortable to be hated. We don't desire it or look for it; but if we decide to follow Him, it will happen. Even when the love of God is moving through you and me, we will face persecution. When we confront sin and evil for the Kingdom's sake, there will be a battle. War is never comfortable.

• Other Reasons We Don't Move in the Gifts

1. Bad theology – Predominately, doctrine that teaches the Gifts were only to establish the Church in the first century, or that only certain Gifts remain today in less supernatural forms.

2. Wrong worldview – Westerners' worldview focuses on the empirical senses and skeptically views the supernatural. Most other worldviews expect the supernatural.

3. Last, but certainly not least, the devil – The devil is a liar. He will fight to keep you from experiencing the supernatural. Once you have seen the power of God move, it is difficult to

turn back to the "average" Christian life. We've, unfortunately, reduced the Christian walk into dos and don'ts and disciplines; but there is more. God is alive and wants to use you to show the world that He is.

We've established a few reasons many choose not to move in the spiritual gifts. Now, why should one really want the Gifts?

1. It's commanded – "Freely you have received, now freely give." To quote an old evangelistic line, "The Great Commission is not The Great Suggestion." It's a part of the Christian life. And He does not want to send you out like sheep among wolves or without first giving you "power over unclean spirits, to cast out and to heal all kinds of sickness and all kinds of disease." (See Matthew 10.)

2. You should want to move in the Gifts of the Holy Spirit because it's something God wants for you to serve His purposes.

3. Because you want to see people come to know Christ – For example, it is easy to lead someone to Christ after you've prayed for them and they are healed.

4. Because you want to see the Kingdom of God established and the enemy defeated – Kingdom warfare is real and fought on a spiritual plane.

5. Because you want to see God's people grow and be blessed.

Dr. Jack Hayford has stated:

"Jesus gave us the gift of the Holy Spirit, yet when the Spirit comes, He is loaded with packages! He desires to release much more in us and through us than we could ever imagine. These gifts are given for delivery, not for accumulation. We receive them to pass them on to others."[19]

There are a lot of good reasons to want the Gifts as expressions in our life. But no reason rises above the primacy of love... A force armed in power and love is being recruited to take ground owned by the enemy.

The Gifts of 1 Corinthians 12 (A Summary)

<u>Context:</u> Paul was writing to the Corinthian church to correct the use of nine specific gifts given by the Holy Spirit. They considered the Gifts as ends in themselves, failing to understand their proper use in the church. They also improperly understood that the Gifts, unlike their pagan counterparts, do not "possess" people, but empower, not overpower. The human will is never negated. All the Gifts, when properly manifested, will bring glory to Christ for "the profit of all."

Purpose: To profit the body (the church). The Greek word *sumphero* means "to bring together, to benefit, to be advantageous." The Gifts are available to every believer as the Spirit gives (1 Corinthians 12:11). They are not to be acknowledged passively, but actively desired; yet they are not received due to merit (1 Corinthians 13:1, 14:1). They are expressions of God's grace at work to fulfill the mission of the Church (1 Corinthians 12:11-27).

Definition: An endowment or supernatural power given by the Holy Spirit.

Greek:

(Please refer to pages 310-312 of *Foundations of Pentecostal Theology*, Revised and Updated Volume 1.)

The New Testament uses six Greek words in reference to spiritual gifts:

Pneumatika – 1 Corinthians 12:1 Often translated "spiritual gifts" (the word "gifts" is not in the original text and so it is written in italics in the NKJV) it literally means "spiritual" or "things of the spirit."

Charismata (plural) – 1 Corinthians 12:4 The word *charis* is Greek and means "grace." A *charisma* (singular) translates "gift" or "spiritual gift." Hence, *charisma* is a "grace gift" given freely by God.[20]

Diakonai – 1 Corinthians 12:5 "There are differences of ministries (*diakonai*)…" Someone who develops a ministry exercising any one of the Gifts may be recognized by fellow believers. Their ministry will always edify the Body and empower the Church to fulfill its mission.

Energemata – 1 Corinthians 12:6 Translated "activities." "The spiritual gifts are activities of the Spirit that produce spiritual effects."[21]

Diairesis – 1 Corinthians 12:4-6 Translated "diversities/differences." The use of this word is to emphasize the distribution of the Gifts. There will be much variety in the way the Gifts are manifested.

Phanerosis – 1 Corinthians 12:7 Translated "manifestations." Every operation of the Gifts is a manifestation of the Spirit. The Holy Spirit is alive and working through believers for the "profit of all."

The List/Summary (in order):[22]

Word of Wisdom: Supernatural perspective for direction, problem solving, means for accomplishing Gods will (will work to compliment other gifts).

Word of Knowledge: Supernatural revelation of God's will and actions of both past and present realities

Gift of Faith: Supernatural ability to believe and trust God in a given situation

Gifts of Healings: Supernatural ability to heal

Gift of Working of Miracles: Supernatural intervention of the laws of nature for the glory of God

Gift of Prophecy: Supernatural utterance to proclaim the will of God

Gift of Discerning of Spirits: Supernatural ability to detect and understand the purpose of various spirits

Gift of Tongues: Supernatural utterance in an unknown language to the speaker – can be a known language, or prayer language, or direct communication to the Holy Spirit

Gift of Interpretation of Tongues: Supernatural ability to know the meaning of the tongues being spoken

Chapter Three

Do We Really Need the Gifts in Today's World?

Driving up the steep, long driveway past the salmon-colored stucco, I felt my stomach wishing to exit my body. For some reason, known only to God, I chose to keep an appointment I'd been dreading for weeks. By mistake, I entered the building through the back door.

Looking much like a man lost in a women's shoe store, I glanced around the rooms and hallways for my appointment: an old friend who offered to meet only if I would come to this place. A nurse, at least I thought her to be a nurse because of the green scrubs she wore, took mercy on me and asked if she could help.

"I'm looking for John Bills. He volunteers here."

"Oh, yes." Her initial enthusiasm gave me hope until she dashed them upon the rocks of my fear-filled heart. "He's not here. Can I help you?"

I muttered something about our meeting and the possibility of me volunteering. Maybe because volunteers were rare (they were) or maybe she took some perverse delight in seeing me in a heightened state of discomfort, either motivation, she literally shared the ground rules and etiquette as she walked me to a room. A waiting room? A lunch room? I could use a very strong cup of coffee.

The room had a number and a single occupant: Brian, as I would soon learn, from Dubuque, Iowa. After her short instructions, she closed the door and left me looking down on a young man in bed who, by any powers of observation, had little time to live.

God Help Me

Under my breath I prayed the prayer both the world and the Church, throughout the ages, have uttered. Profound in its simplicity and rich in its emotion, "God, help me," as I extended my hand to shake his. But Brian couldn't move. He was, in fact, breathing some of his last breaths. Yet his demeanor was strangely bright, almost optimistic.

Brian was dying from AIDS in an AIDS hospice in the hills of Los Angeles, across from the police academy. And I was now a volunteer, and would be so every week for the next two years. I never did see John Bills.

I tell this long story to open this chapter because it taught me a critical life lesson in Kingdom living. In the next two years, volunteering at an AIDS hospice run by gay activists who were extremely angry with the Church (I learned this later in my time there) the clash of kingdoms became very real. Every

If we grow in love, we gain God's heart for the real reason He asks us to desire the gifts.

time I entered its doors the battle raged, and it forced me to use the gifts of the Spirit. Yet, none of those Gifts would have any meaning had I not loved both patients and staff alike. Love did conquer all; but both power and love combined gave me the ability to take ground in the enemy's camp. Not that the staff or the patients were the adversary, to say so would be to miss the point entirely. Many, in fact, became friends; but the hospice needed the presence of God to come and to be established – on earth as it is in heaven.

We forget that the "Love Chapter" of 1 Corinthians 13 is written in context of 1 Corinthians 12:31, "Earnestly desire the best gifts," and 14:1, "Desire spiritual gifts." It is love that embraces the power of God for the purpose of establishing God's will and not our own. If we grow in love, we gain God's heart for the real reason He asks us to desire the gifts.

I'm convinced God is calling all of us to go to those places we fear the most. Not so much so that we conquer fear itself, but so that we go in our weakness, knowing He must be strong through us. And His love will be manifested – not more of our weak and ineffectual attempts at love.

For me, at that moment during the height of the AIDS crisis, it was a hospice at a particularly spiritually poor time in my life – but not for long; for there's nothing like a battle to set you right. It may be crossing the street to a belligerent neighbor, or having coffee with the extended family member you always avoid at Christmas. Being in battle, however big or small, tests your mettle. It has a way of clarifying motives and shaking up complacency – but only if the motive for the battle is love.

Walking in the Spirit, armed with the Gifts, clothed in love is the "right stuff" needed for those desiring to take back chunks of enemy territory.

The Camps

The Charismatic/Pentecostal churches that I speak at around the world seem to be increasingly divided into two camps in regard to the gifts of the Holy Spirit.

Camp One – This camp doesn't deny the Gifts, they just tend to ignore them. At times, it seems they are either embarrassed by or just choose to not promote their use.

Whether it's the lack of cool or the "weirdness" factor that seems to especially trouble the younger pastors, or those that have experienced abuses and feel it's simply not worth the trouble – either way, there is a growing apathy or antipathy. The Church need not choose between social activism and spiritual activism. Pastors often struggle to find balance between the two, usually emphasizing that which they are most comfortable with – a dangerous reason to choose.

Two – These folks believe in the Gifts and really want to exercise them in church life. Pastors and members alike will come up to me after a sermon or conference and say, "Oh, if we could get back to the book of Acts." Yes, it's as if something is holding them back. They see some healing, hear some prophecy, but nothing has truly impacted their church, let alone their community.

In my opinion, where they tend to miss it is seeing the Gifts as only blessing the Church and not the community. And when they see the Gifts as God's grace to the world, they begin to see everyone in the church as a minister of the gospel – a church-altering paradigm shift.

A Third Way – What I love to share with both "camps" is that the Gifts, if properly exercised and people properly commissioned, can and will bring both together. The Gifts are grace-given by God to believers to bless the saved and unsaved, rich and poor, millennial, Generation X, Y, or Z, to Baby Boomers and beyond. The Gifts also cross racial and class lines, something desperately needed in today's world. Seeing people set free of bondage, healed from disease, and delivered from darkness is a common denominator of humanity.

An old man once told me he had interviewed two African-American women in the 1940s about what they witnessed during the Azusa Street Revival. Their answer to the question of their greatest experience surprised him. He expected a story about healing or prayer or some supernatural event. Instead, the two women agreed that the most amazing testimony of God's presence during that period was that people of many races stayed after the services and shared

> The power of God will not only heal the blind, it will open our eyes to others' hurt and pain.

together in a potluck of food – a big, big deal in those days… and unfortunately, even today in many circles.

The power of God will not only heal the blind, it will open our eyes to others' hurt and pain. It will open our ears to hear what the Spirit is truly saying through the Word.

> *There is neither Jew nor Greek, there is neither slave nor free, there is neither male nor female; for you are all one in Christ Jesus.* Galatians 3:28

The Gifts are Very "Book of Acts"

What do I mean?

> *But you shall receive power when the Holy Spirit has come upon you; and you shall be witnesses to Me in Jerusalem, and in all Judea and Samaria, and to the end of the earth.* Acts 1:8

A resurrected Jesus promises the disciples that they would receive power. Not just any power, but power from the Holy Spirit. In so doing, this power would transform them into witnesses of His new covenant. A fearful band of believers would soon have the "juice" to take on, literally, the world. They would be the first "woke" generation – as we will see.

Jesus' choice in Acts 1:8 of where they would witness is not random or arbitrary; it had meaning to those who sat there staring at the Master in wonder.

1. **Jerusalem** – Start your witness at home: your family and friends. If it's not real here, don't take your weak witness elsewhere. And remember, evangelism isn't merely a plan or a strategy, but living life filled in the Spirit and having that dynamic life spill over in word and deed.

2. **All Judea** – It's more than just your private religion; it's a message for all. Many unreached people groups lived in Judea. Jesus was telling them that their witness of all He did must go to rich, poor, unclean, and many ostracized people groups that had come to their land to live. Today, almost every nation has the opportunity to reach out and love the immigrant community. That is not to dismiss civil law or cultural challenges, but the highest law in God's Kingdom is love.

3. **Samaria** – This probably rattled some cages. Samaritans were the despised people, considered worse than even the Romans. By sending them there, Jesus was in fact saying, confront your prejudice, your ignorance, your intolerance, because the power of God must go to all people – like it or not. Can you imagine a church that tackles the big societal

issues with radical compassion and honest love? But most of all, modeling that compassion – an army of evangelical, Spirit-filled Mother Teresas!

4. **To the Ends of the Earth** – This was probably not even on the disciples' radar. Acts 2:6 indicates that they were still focused on some kind of earthly kingdom in Israel. I've found, over the years, good churches and Spirit-filled pastors fight unwittingly to keep the focus on their church, their people, and their community. Jesus' last point of ministry forces us to care, give, even go when we may see absolutely nothing in return. The Kingdom of God has no borders and only cares about God's purposes. It's hard to argue with Oswald J. Smith who once said:

"No one has the right to hear the gospel twice, while there remains someone who has not heard it once."

Jesus is giving the ultimate "Think Big" sermon. He's empowering to establish the Kingdom of God – in every sector of every culture in the world. Over the years I have seen God enter into the most depraved hearts coming from a truly darkened culture, and just as powerfully change the most intellectual sophisticate. There are no boundaries from God, but we seem to erect them.

Referring to Acts 1:8, Dr. Paul Pierson, former president of Fuller Seminary, wrote:

"These words symbolized the breaking of an almost infinite number of barriers in order that men and women everywhere might hear and respond to the Good News."[1]

He goes on with this great insight:

"Just as God in Christ had broken through the barriers which separated eternity from time, divinity from humanity, holiness from sin, so his people were to break through geographical, racial, linguistic, religious, cultural, and social barriers in order that people of every race and tongue might receive the Good News."[2]

And as the late C. Peter Wagner, renowned church growth expert, responded to his boss's quote appropriately:

"But it could not be implemented with human power alone... three years with Jesus Himself had only partially equipped them for what was ahead. They needed much more than that to engage in the spiritual warfare necessary to take the Kingdom by force (see Matthew 11:12)."[3]

Do You See It?

In Acts 1, Jesus preaches the big sermon; but it wasn't until Acts 2 and the wind of Pentecost that He transfers the power and responsibility for the Kingdom of God to His followers. It would take the same Holy Spirit that authorized His ministry to baptize those very followers. But before their in-filling, He told them the hard truth – this Kingdom is not just for them, but for the whole world: *panta ta ethne*, every people group.

> It's tongues-speaking while feeding the poor. It's prophesying hope over the prostitute.

Acts 1:8, combined with the power to achieve it in Acts 2, is the so-called "social gospel," plus missions and evangelism, with Holy Ghost revival, in one verse! It's tongues-speaking while feeding the poor. It's prophesying hope over the prostitute. It's healing the sick, then sharing the gospel with them. And it's giving the disenfranchised not only the gospel of redemption, but with power.

It's Kingdom of God stuff – on earth as it is in heaven.

My message to the two camps: His power is for all, to all. Don't only give bread to the hungry; lead them into an Acts 2 encounter that gives clarity of purpose with power. Sometimes we fall into the so-called soft bigotry of low expectations. We expect little from those saved from difficult conditions; yet, they can be the most powerful of God's instruments. Who can reach the lost the best? Someone radically found! Who can speak to the down and out, the hurting, the suffering? Those who know the pain firsthand – YET, have found the answer.

El Sim

My good friend, Ted Olbrich, a nation changer whose ministry in Cambodia is literally seeing a Buddhist nation become a Christian one, recently told the story of one of his greatest leaders in this extraordinary people movement.

One of the many converts in Cambodia wanted to share his faith using a boat to go along the numerous riverbanks that snake through this South East Asia nation – a country still healing from a genocidal maniac, the dictator, Pol Pot. Ted approved the mission and the boat. The zealous worker took off, only to stop when he saw a woman washing her clothes by the bank of the river. This was a completely unreached island region, so the worker wasted no time in explaining the gospel to her.

Her name was El Sim and she would become famous in the region, the first convert in this isolated island. At four feet six inches, her diminutive stature and plain physical appearance belied the powerful nature of her future ministry. Both poor and illiterate, soon El Sim, full of the Holy Spirit, began to share Christ with the villagers. The gospel of grace held a fascination to these Buddhists who believed that their lives on earth determined their reincarnated futures. The message of Jesus was a freedom from the past and a hope for not only the future, but also the reality of the present. In a culture where suffering is as expected as breathing, the Good News came to a hungry people.

Yet, when a disease swept through the region killing thousands, including El Sim's 12-year-old daughter, despite her loss, she persevered – continuing to preach the gospel, caring for the sick, praying for their healing. People saw her boldness and responded.

Her other younger, surviving daughter, Ruthie, was sickly since birth. After numerous doctor visits, they diagnosed Leukemia and proceeded with a bone marrow transplant. It failed. A second one failed too. This little girl grew sicker and eventually died.

Upon hearing the news, Ted Olbrich contacted El Sim's district supervisor, a Cambodian, and in his often blunt, irreverent manner told him, "This is bad advertising... go there and say something, do something." Ted knew that in losing two daughters, not only would El Sim need encouragement, but her ministry might be in peril if villagers considered her faith lacked power in a world full of power encounters.

Ruthie's body, which had been dead for 20 hours, lay wrapped in straw mats. The district supervisor, arriving for the funeral, kneeled before the dead little girl. Laying his hand on the straw, he prayed not for healing or a resurrection, but for words to share that would bring both comfort and understanding to a bewildered people. Some 500 had gathered.

As he prayed, he felt another hand upon his; El Sim had joined him in prayer. What happened next I only include in this book because I so trust my friend, Ted. "Ruthie jumped up out of the straw mats and said, 'Oh, Wow!' then began to describe her time in heaven in detail."

El Sim's first words to her supervisor, "How come you never told me of the God who raises the dead?"

More signs and wonders began to follow. The remaining Buddhists could not deny the power of the Christian God. According to Ted, El Sim "went on to work every miracle of the book of Acts – several times."

Hers was not only a ministry of power, but of compassion, both for the body and the soul. She baptized over 50,000 people, built water wells (after being directed to the water by the Holy Spirit), opened businesses for the people, created healthcare, and of course, cared for the widows and orphans. El Sim, a simple, poor, illiterate woman became the model Kingdom warrior. She depended only on the Holy Spirit to lead her. She listened for the voice of her Master and spoke what she heard Him say.

"My sheep hear my voice." In a world where believers try to listen, the static of the world, even of their own unbelief, turns the volume of God's voice down. Not so with El Sim. Her ear heard clearly what the Spirit was saying. And just as importantly, if not more, she obeyed. People came from different nations to see what God was doing through her. Though growing in fame and stature, she lived simply, continuing to love her people. A Mother Teresa with Holy Ghost power.

If her story could only end there...

But as with most real life stories, with no Hollywood scriptwriter, her life had no neat, tidy, fairytale ending. El Sim's husband became jealous of her growing fame, numerous speaking engagements, and contact with Western leaders. When she disappeared, he accused her of "running off" with a missionary; but the truth would be revealed. He murdered her in a fit of rage.

How could it be? Ted felt the loss as strongly as if it was his own child. The Lord reminded him of the real life struggle that is not of flesh and blood, but of principalities and power. The Bible says the devil comes to kill, destroy, and steal. We are in a death match with the devil and sometimes he wins a battle, though certainly not the war.

Early Church father, Tertullian, rightfully stated:

"The blood of the martyrs is the seed of the church."

We need a fearless group of Kingdom ambassadors who do not shrink from a war with darkness.

Chapter Four

Do We Really Need the Gifts? – Part 2

One day they came to my school – fresh-faced, white shirts, black pants and ties. Let's just say they stood out in a world of bell-bottoms and tie-dye shirts. They told me there was more than the Bible, more than what corrupt Christianity offered. I was intrigued. After a cordial, if not pleasant, exchange, they challenged me to take their book, read it, and then guaranteed that I would have a "witness," a kind of burning-in-the-bosom experience that would prove its authenticity, and that their prophet was God's prophet. This was an experience my Baptist church never spoke about.

I took the book home and began to read it. Then I did something after about an hour of reading, something probably only new believers, who know very little, get to do. I asked the Lord to show me in the Bible if what I was reading was truth or not. Not knowing where to start, I asked the Lord to guide me, directly, to the verse or verses that contained His answer.

Randomly, I opened my Bible, closed my eyes, and put my finger on a verse, hoping it would bring divine clarity. Matthew 7:15 spoke loud and clear:

Beware of false prophets...

Now I had a witness. This experience was also my initial experience, after conversion, of the supernatural. God could and would speak to us, directly, if we asked Him to do so.

It also taught me a fundamental lesson. If we share our faith with anyone else, we must believe it ourselves. We need to have a "witness" inside our heart and mind and to believe the Bible is absolutely true. We must be open to see the God of the Bible work within our spirit to guide us into all truth.

> My faith seemed much less an intellectual acknowledgment of sacred history and more like a daring adventure.

But when he, the Spirit of truth, comes, he will guide you into all truth. John 16:13

This new life called Christianity involved much more than memorizing Bible verses. There was the "strange" third person of the Trinity that promised to "help" me along the way. My faith seemed much less an intellectual acknowledgment of sacred history and more like a daring adventure. I didn't just join a church, I signed up for a purpose – beyond me. I really didn't know it at the time, but I had enlisted in the Army of God.

God's Army

Any military person will tell you that nothing gets them prepared like an upcoming battle. War is sobering. It takes multiple individuals trained and given proper weapons to join as one force to overcome the strategies of the enemy.

The U.S. Marines have a motto that unifies and identifies them as a special branch of the military, "Semper Fidelis," or "Semper Fi" – always faithful.

God's army also has distinctives – like baptism in water and in the Holy Spirit. Each one is to have a witness, a personal testimony that the Holy Spirit "has come upon you." And they shall receive power and a commission to make disciples according to the strategy set out by Jesus in Acts 1:8.

Jesus clearly indicated that every believer has been commissioned and given the tools to achieve the task. No Marine would leave their rifle behind when going into battle. Why is it so many believers forget the "weapons of our warfare"?

One of my good friends in Papua New Guinea tells a story of his aunt, an actual witch, from an island absolutely filled with witchcraft. Despite his aunt's occupation, she still loves him and accepts him because he is family. On one of his visits, during a friendly conversation with her, she laughed a bit and said, "You Christians are so funny. If you really knew how powerful it is when you pray, you would pray so much more."

Boot Camp for Believers

Of course, the nine gifts this book is focusing on are only a portion of the weapons available to the believer. Like the well-trained individual in the military, the weapons in the hands of someone who lacks character or moral compass can be disastrous. Boot camp, for any military branch, focuses on fundamentals, including use of weaponry; but even more fundamental is the essential to follow orders from above and to learn to trust your fellow comrades. Otherwise, chaos and breakdown ensue, the battle is lost, and the enemy will come to plunder.

Becoming a Super Soldier

As stated before, there is divine wisdom in following 1 Corinthians 12 with the Love Chapter (1 Corinthians 13). Paul makes it abundantly clear that gifts without the fruit is folly – especially the fruit of love.

And though I have the gift of prophecy, and understand all mysteries and all knowledge, and though I have all faith, so that I could remove mountains, but have not love, I am nothing. I Corinthians 13:2

The fruit of the Spirit come gradually from our inner person. Like any plant, you can't make it grow faster or even speed up the fruit bearing process. Fruit shows us, and others, the character of God. The Gifts show His power. The two working together make for a super soldier.

We don't have to choose between one or the other; both blessings are available. Paul says it best:

Pursue love, and desire spiritual gifts... 1 Corinthians 14:1

Be hungry for both. Character and power make for an effective witness. Jesus obviously had both and desired His disciples to have each. He knew that winning the world following the divine strategy of Acts 1:8 required both.

However, without question, those who move in the Gifts but ignore or de-emphasize the fruit are in for trouble. The church in Corinth understood this well. Power not rooted in love will grow into pride. We know where that leads – the fall. However, love is a powerful force; it never fails.

Add joy, peace, longsuffering, kindness, goodness, faithfulness, gentleness, and self-control (Galatians 5:22-23) and you possess character that the world cannot duplicate. Yet, these characteristics, like the Gifts, come from the Spirit. He produces them over time within you.

The Lesson from the Fruit Tree

There was a tree that taught me a very valuable lesson some years ago when we were pastoring in Southern California. We had purchased a typical tract home from the 1950s growth era. An older gentleman who was born and raised there told me that much of the area was originally an orange tree orchard. One of those original orange trees was still left in the backyard of our new home.

At first I didn't pay it much attention; but within a few months or so I noticed oranges beginning to grow all over this tree – not just a few, but what looked like hundreds of huge navel oranges. The tree produced so many that the limbs were literally hanging down and some almost touching the ground. At first we thought this was wonderful; but as time went on, oranges and oranges and oranges kept coming out of that tree.

I actually began getting annoyed with all the oranges that kept growing out of this old tree. Why would anyone be annoyed at such a wonderful, healthy, fruitful tree? The oranges were always fantastic. But what bothered me was that our family could only eat so many oranges. So, my wife always gave me the task of bagging them all up and then trying to find people to give them to.

Every time a new orange crop was coming on that tree, I knew work for me was on the way. That meant climbing up into that huge tree, which was always filled with dirty branches and spiders. This was not at all the kind of thing that this sophisticated preacher wanted to do. But what a lesson God taught me through that old orange tree.

> But the fruit of the Spirit is love, joy, peace, patience, kindness, goodness, faithfulness, gentleness, self-control; against such things there is no law. Galatians 5:22-23

One day, a revelation came that left me in awe of the power of God that works in us. You see, it is the Holy Spirit's power, the same Spirit that raised Christ from the dead, that produces the fruit of the Spirit in you. If you want more love, joy, peace, patience, kindness, goodness, faithfulness, gentleness, and self-control, develop a sensitivity to the Holy Spirit, and He will produce His fruit in your life.

That orange tree had no choice but to bear awesome fruit, because it was a tree planted in the most ideal soil and climate for growing oranges. After all, we were in the city of Garden

Grove in Orange County, California. Of course that tree was going to produce fruit in a city and a county with names like that!

How easy it is to bear the fruit of the Spirit when you are plugged into the river of the Spirit and He is flowing in and out of your life. I have found that when I am full of the Spirit I am always more loving, more joyful, more patient, more kind, full of goodness and faithfulness, more gentle, and absolutely more self-controlled.

Because the fruit is who you are; the gifts are what you share.

Jesus said we could evaluate a person based on the fruit in their life, not necessarily by the gifts. Why? Because the fruit is who you are; the gifts are what you share. In God's plan we can have both, by the Spirit.

Let's seek a beautiful balance between gifts and fruit. Let Him build character from within and give you power from without. Fruit of the Spirit will protect you from pride and jealousy or envy – "If only I had their gift!"

Are the Gifts for Everyone?

Can any believer move in all the Gifts?

This is probably the most disputed of questions relating to the believer moving in the gifts of the Holy Spirit. Here is the short answer: YES.

Here is the more thoughtful, scriptural answer:

Nowhere in Scripture does it say the Gifts (specifically the nine referred to in 1 Corinthians 12) are not for all believers. They (the Gifts) are distributed through the Church at His will – the phrase "to each one" or "to one" or "to another" in verses 7, 8, 9, 10, and 11 does not mean each gift is given exclusively to that one at the exclusion of another. It simply means what it says: The Holy Spirit bestows the Gifts to whom He wills as the occasion arises (verse 11).

A key point is that everyone is involved – everyone who is willing to be used by the Holy Spirit for His purposes.

> *Now to each one the manifestation of the Spirit is given for the common good.* 1 Corinthians 12:7

This, in a real sense, is protection from a belief that the Gifts are given exclusively to some. Instead, "gift giving" by the Holy Spirit is dynamic and we can expect Him to move through us in multiple ways.

After listing the nine gifts in 1 Corinthians 12:8-10, Paul concludes in verse 11:

But one and the same Spirit works all these things,
distributing to each one individually as He wills.

These are clear statements of the supernatural quality (not a heightened natural ability) of the Gifts, and the sense that the Gifts are given to us by the Spirit to fulfill specific yet multiple purposes.

"The Holy Spirit bestows the Gifts to whom He wills as the occasion recommends from the divine view point."[1]

Focus on verse 7, the phrase "each one." Notice he didn't say to leaders, or pastors, or TV evangelists (couldn't resist) or only for special anointed types, or only older, seasoned Christians who know the Bible inside and out. NO! Each one. That means you and me if we love Jesus.

In 1 Corinthians 12:31 and again in 14:1, Paul tells his readers to "desire" the Gifts. Why would he do so if you were not to participate in them? It would be cruel to encourage someone to desire something they could not have. And, note he didn't limit you to just one gift.

Without question, Paul believed that operating in the Gifts is essential to the health of the Church. Yet, the church in Corinth needed guidelines and an understanding of the proper motivation.

Since you are zealous for Spiritual gifts (note the plural) *let it be for the edification of the church that you seek to excel.*
1 Corinthians 14:12

In 1 Corinthians 14, Paul sets forth basic principles concerning the use of the Gifts listed earlier in his letter. Among these principles he states in verse 31:

For you can all prophesy one by one that all may learn and all may be encouraged.

All means all. This is of course different than the office of the prophet, which Paul mentions in 12:28, 29. Not all operate as a God-appointed prophet in the church, but all can prophesy. Just as not all are called to the office of an evangelist, pastor, or teacher, yet we all can and should share the gospel, care for people, and teach others.

Let's be open to how the Holy Spirit wants to bestow His gifts on us.

The Issue Within

The real issue facing the Church today isn't if the Gifts are for today, or for you. The real challenge is helping the believer truly believe that the Gifts are for them and then receive them into their lives.

Here is a statement you may feel incapable of saying or unworthy to speak out loud: "I am gifted by God. I have the gifts of the Holy Spirit ready to flow out of me."

Quick sidebar, lest saying something so affirmative and true concerns you – maybe it's because the enemy of your soul has been lying to you. I can't begin to tell of all the "Christian soldiers" lying in a MASH unit – sidelined from the Kingdom battle because they've believed in one or more demonic lies.

"I'm not worthy." None of us are, but our God is, and He made you not only worthy, but He has made you a son or daughter, His ambassador (representing Him and His Kingdom). Get that in your spirit, in your mind and emotions, and I promise the impact you will have and the joy you will know will amaze you.

Well-known minister to abused and trafficked youth, and person who has overcome a deep sense of her own unworthiness, Christine Caine, wrote:

"The devil is a liar but never forget that he is a very loud liar. You must choose to turn off his voice by turning up the voice of God."[2]

Gia

Gia is a tall, strong woman with jet-black hair framing equally black eyes, mother of four grown boys, wife of a fireman, and minister of the gospel.

Born and raised within the sounds and confines of Ike and Tina Turner's music studio in Inglewood, California, Gia's early life was comprised of hugs from Wolfman Jack and smiles from Al Green. But by age eight, Gia's parents divorced. As dysfunctional as her family had been, life truly shattered when her mother remarried.

Eight years of sexual abuse at the hands of her stepfather and the imprisonment of her mother left Gia in a world of survival.

In the middle of this chaos, a neighbor invited her to a Bible Study led by charismatic Catholics. Though the idea of studying the Bible proved to be as foreign to her as a trustworthy male figure, this time with believers left a powerful impression.

It took a simple prayer to push Gia along the path to discovering Christ. She got on her knees as an 18-year-old and cried out to God, "If you're really there, send someone to love me, not hurt me."

A blind date with a kind young man named Shawn would be the answered prayer Gia hoped for. They were soon married. They still are today after 31 years.

Four sons later, Gia still felt empty and lost. Her journey led her to work for a company owned by Orthodox Jews whose employees reflected the spectrum of beliefs from Wiccan to Mormonism. One of these employees, a Christian, felt led to pray for her, and with Easter coming, she decided to go to church, taking her boys.

During the altar call, she walked forward, receiving prayer and a touch from God. She left with an insatiable hunger for God's Word – soaking it in every day. One day, while reading it out loud, a strange language pressed through her lips. She screamed out, "Oh my God, I'm possessed!" It was a full language that she did not know or understand.

Because of her lack of knowledge, she stopped speaking in it and according to her own estimation, "I lived 15 years of powerless Christianity," sharing time in both the world and the church. "I did the splits," Gia colorfully recalled.

It would take a life and death health battle with Lyme Disease, lesions on the brain, and a doctor's proclamation, "We can't do anything for you," to cause Gia to cling to her faith.

A friend and prayer warrior finally prophesied over Gia, "It's time to be healed." Laying hands on her head, pain immediately left her body – all except one little pain on her neck. Her friend, operating in a word of wisdom, told her to pray for that spot. When the pain left, it served as an encouragement for Gia to also pray and believe for healing for others.

Life would never be the same. No more "splits." The Word of God came alive, with the Holy Spirit giving her insights reserved for biblical scholars. All nine gifts of the Spirit were a part of Gia's ministry arsenal.

During prayer for a blind woman, the Lord gave her instructions to "spit in her eyes." Silently protesting the Lord's command, she relented, saying humbly to the woman and the other prayer partners, "The Lord is telling me to put spit in your eyes." Instead of the anticipated protest, everyone in unison said, "Do it!"

The blind woman was completely healed.

Gia's life scars have allowed her to better understand and relate to the pain of so many. Yet, even today, she still sees herself as a work in progress. "I can minister to others, but struggle at times believing it myself."

As she seeks God for deeper personal healing, she remains a Kingdom warrior. Her growth is based on a fundamental trust in the person of the Holy Spirit to teach her and empower her.

God is exceedingly doing both.

Chapter Five

So What Do I Have to Do to Receive the Spiritual Gifts?

They held the promise close to their hearts. It brought them a peace so desperately needed. Though they had seen him resurrected and taken up into the clouds, the promise answered their very real, very human questions: What is next? What do we do now?

They gathered upstairs, no longer filled in fear, but in anticipation of a future adventure. No thoughts of going on their own or going back to a previous life. They knew life would never be the same and that they were part of something very special – they were chosen to be his witnesses.

But first, they must wait. Actively wait. They came together as one, praying, pressing in – like D-Day soldiers waiting to storm the beaches at Normandy.

The promise was power to do battle. So they positioned themselves to receive, together in the upper room.

Be in Position

So what should I do to position myself to receive and move in the spiritual Gifts?

What position were the first disciples in, waiting in the upper room? Besides introspection and extreme anticipation, they were desperate for God...

1. **Be in a position of hunger for the things of God.**

   Can you imagine the prayers, the cries to God by those waiting in the upper room? What if we, the Church, would be willing to forsake everything for a touch from Him? Here's part of my story:

   "What ever happened to the guy who would cry out for the things of God?"

   Everyone starts as equals when it comes to seeking Him. How you grow is up to you!

   My wife didn't really expect a reply. But she knew her rhetorical question would burrow deep into my soul. It did. Our life had become comfortable. Why mess with it? Nice church. Good attendance. People tithed. What more could a pastor want?

   More of God.

As long as I can remember, my spiritual life has always been captivated by a deep desire to know God and to experience all He has for me. A valuable life lesson learned: There will always be more gifted, smarter, more educated people in the Kingdom than you. But, everyone starts as equals when it comes to seeking Him. How you grow is up to you!

> *But seek first the kingdom of God and His righteousness, and all these things shall be added to you.* Matthew 6:33

No verse sums it up better. As we put God and the things of God first, life will find its truest meaning and you will find ultimate purpose and joy.

You will also discover the gifts of the Spirit.

My wife challenged me out of love. She knew that even though times were good, and we were living a comfortable but God-fearing life, it wasn't enough for me or for her.

So, I soaked up all I could read about the revivals of the 18th, 19th, and early 20th centuries. The great men and women of faith – the Smith Wigglesworths and Aimee Semple McPhersons modeled the Spirit-filled life in early post Azusa Street. Of course, many more followed. I'd read every book, listened to every cassette tape (Google it, my millennial friends ☺) by my heroes in the faith.

A hunger for more and more of the presence and power of God began to stir in me; and the more I consumed seemed to make me even hungrier. Really, I just couldn't get enough. What was it that these incredible leaders took hold of that ushered in such times of power and the life-transforming presence of the Lord?

What was the common denominator that each shared? Without question, each was gifted by God, both naturally and supernaturally. But, what brought them to the highest level in Kingdom living? An unquenchable thirst for God and His Kingdom.

Are you satisfied by what this world can offer you? A happy marriage, loving children, a comfortable home, and rewarding job? Be honest. Living the safe, comfortable life is the path most believers take, especially in America.

My church was growing, our lives were rewarding, and I had found temporary satisfaction in all these good things – until she reminded me what I knew deep down inside. I knew that if I was not as passionate about the things of God as I once was, I had back-slidden.

.... for the Son of Man has come to seek and to save that which was lost. **Luke 19:10**

My priority had to change.

Salvation is such a rich word in the Bible. It is much more than souls escaping the fires of hell. The word can include rescue, deliverance, and preservation, but also soundness, prosperity, happiness, and general well being.

My mission aligned with Jesus' mission: to bring the fullness of salvation, to retake that which the enemy of our souls tries to steal and destroy, and to give us abundant life.

> *The thief does not come except to steal, and to kill, and to destroy. I have come that they may have life, and that they may have it more abundantly.* John 10:10

What's Not Working While Eating the Snacks

Good friend, Cere Muscarella, the senior pastor of an exceptional church in Texas, believes that hunger is the critical starting point. If one is truly hungry for the things of God, according to Cere, they will allow the Holy Spirit to honestly, deeply search what in their life is not working.

In fact, his ministry took a radical turn when he asked his church staff to evaluate him. Already successful and on a trajectory for even larger growth, Cere was admittedly "bored," but the staff's collective opinions changed that rapidly.

"I was really looking forward to pages of encouragement and for course corrections, when they handed me a nicely bound folder.

"Instead, I knew I was in trouble when they told me, 'Brother, we want you to know we really love you and prayed about everything in here.'"

The "book" he received was the exact opposite of what he expected and the evaluation devastated, yet brought freedom.

One of the many Holy Spirit inspired insights that would revolutionize his ministry was this need for absolute hunger for God.

"To develop a true hunger for God you need to recognize that we may be distracted by the 'snacks' that fill us just enough, but leave us short of complete submission to the Spirit."

Speaking with Cere on this subject, I thought of the many "snacks" that partially satisfied my soul but pushed me away from the real banquet dinner – all that the Lord has for us if we will open the door and dine with Him. Maybe you will too.

2. **Be in a position to receive from the Word of God.**

Pressing in to become the person God can use to expand His Kingdom means becoming a student of the Word – a serious student. It includes knowing context, history, culture, even nuances of grammar and language. But it also means memorizing God's Word and the ability to share a timely "word" from the Scriptures when appropriate.

The late Dick Mills was one of the prophetic giants of the 20th century, literally touching hundreds of thousands of individuals over his prolific ministry. Nearly every word he gave revolved around the Scriptures.

To move in the Gifts, especially prophecy, one must "handle accurately the word of truth." (2 Timothy 2:15) No shortcuts are allowed.

But it all starts with getting the Word of God not only in your head, but also in your heart. It is an interesting phenomenon in the body of Christ, the lack of balance between intellectual pursuit and the spiritual, even emotional embrace of the Scripture. There has to be a determination to study the Word not only with our minds, but also through the Spirit, allowing Him to teach us. Many well-intentioned believers never seem to properly integrate the two. John Wimber has said:

"The Word of God without the Spirit of God, we dry up; the Spirit of God without the Word of God, we blow up; but the Word of God with the Spirit of God, we grow up."[1]

For the word of God is living and powerful, and sharper than any two-edged sword, piercing even to the division of soul and spirit, and of joints and marrow, and is a discerner of the thoughts and intents of the heart.

Hebrews 4:12

I told a story in my first book, *Positioned for Miracles*, about preaching a sermon in my church in Southern California. I delivered this sermon with as much passion as personally possible. Near the end of the message, working toward an altar-filling climax, a middle-aged woman seated next to the center aisle pulled out her car keys and began jingling them. When I looked at her, she turned to look back at the clock to tell me that lunch couldn't wait and I was running late. The altars were empty that morning.

Later that evening, as I boarded my flight to Vietnam, still stewing over her keys, I read where I'd been asked to preach the same sermon, that seemingly failed, to the Vietnamese leaders. I hesitated to do so, thinking they would respond like the people in my church did. They didn't. All began to cry out to God for over an hour – each repenting deeply.

That week, I also shared many miracle stories and received an unusual response from one of the students. "Pastor, you don't need to tell so many of those miracle stories. We like them, but we experience miracles everyday. What we don't have is Bible teachers like yourself that will come and teach us the Word of God. So please just teach us the Bible. This is what we are the most desperate for."

The lesson learned has never been forgotten: You can let the Word change you, or tickle your ears – it all depends on how hungry you are. (Pun intended to the woman who jingled the keys.)

3. **Be in a position to serve God.**

    Have you ever met someone who seems to have a hotline to God, knows all the right Scriptures, but is accountable to no one? The depth of their "spirituality" negates the need for church life. It's a kind of charismatic butterfly existence – sipping the nectar of the Spirit church-to-church, conference-to-conference! (Yes, I'm being sarcastic.)

    You should be serving in a Bible believing fellowship. Remember 1 Corinthians 12. The context is clearly the church – end of story. Service, though not exclusively, should flow out of life in the community of fellow believers. Every person I have ever encountered that moves powerfully in the Gifts always started in the church or an outreach from the church.

> The fruit of the Spirit is for you, but the Gifts are for the Body of Christ.

This is a key that we'll keep repeating: The gifts of the Spirit in you are not for you. The manifestation of the Spirit is for the common good. In other words, God showing up through you is to bless others. The fruit of the Spirit is for you, but the Gifts are for the Body of Christ. If you ever confuse that you'll get into trouble. Please be aware that as you move in the Gifts, people will naturally be inclined to elevate you and seek you out. Guard your heart with all diligence.

Remember Jesus Himself when sharing from Isaiah in Luke 4:18, *The Spirit of the Lord has anointed me to bring...* We are gifted "to bring" the Good News to the poor, freedom to the captive, recovery of sight to the blind – to establish the Kingdom. Pastor Bill Johnson said it best:

> "The Holy Spirit is in me for my sake, but he is upon me for yours."[2]

4. Be in a position of praise.

Few things open our spirit to the heart and mind of Christ better than pure uninhibited worship. And don't let the fear of man and what others may think stop you from worshiping your creator the way you know is most intimate. Remember David dancing before the Lord and how it embarrassed his wife, Michal. She became barren as a result. May we never become barren in our worship and then in our ministry.

If you've never raised your hands in a posture of surrender, I highly encourage you to do so. There is something very freeing in an unashamed, physical response to your Abba Father. It's like saying, "Pick me up, Daddy!"

Or maybe you've never vocalized praise to God. Start in the privacy of your own home – but start. The Bible is full of scriptures that encourage various physical postures in praise and also vocalizing praise in public. God, of course, knows us well and He knows how important it is to not only give mental acknowledgment, but also a physical response. Remember, like water baptism or communion, often there is a physical connection to a spiritual truth.

Positioning yourself for the presence of God almost always involves praising Him. The Old Testament is replete with stories of praise ranging from a weapon of warfare to the action of a repentant heart.

Enter into his gates with thanksgiving and into his courts with praise... **Psalm 100:4**

Praise, especially in the midst of a difficult situation, establishes the atmosphere with faith rather than fear or unbelief. It is also important in positioning yourself to move in the Gifts. When you don't know what to do, praise Him. If you think you know what to do, praise Him.

The following story from good friend and former Foursquare missionary, Greg Fisher, tells of the power in praise.

"Our first church was in Snoqualmie, Washington – a small town. We were simple, but very sincere people. I had a little Bible College, but a lot of zeal. Our first Sunday we had seven people, six of which were mentally disabled. This small community thought of us as the crazy church – no respect whatsoever. Yet, early on I sensed God clearly say, 'Don't look at anything, I'm going to do something.'

"We worked hard, and in time the church grew to 30 people. My wife, Margaret, and I were amazed. I had learned how to tap into praise and worship, so with our tiny congregation we tapped into heaven on earth and the presence of God came.

"Soon we ballooned to 60 people. Maybe this caught the enemy's attention, because one night an evil presence paid our home a visit. In the middle of a quiet Washington evening, I woke up sensing a presence in our bedroom. I knew it wasn't the Lord. I didn't want this thing to be near my wife, so I got out of bed and commanded it to leave.

"Though not audible, the reply came clearly, 'Stop this ministry, stop teaching people to worship, or I will take your wife from you.'

"I knew just enough about my authority as a believer to reply, 'No, you're not. You can't!'

"The presence moved to our four-year-old daughter's room and spoke again, 'If you don't stop, I'll kill your daughter.'

"I picked her up in my arms and rebuked this demon by singing *I will praise him, praise the Lamb for sinners slain.* The presence fled and my daughter never even woke up.

"The next Sunday at our church, a middle-aged lady, a schoolteacher, asked for prayer. At that time in my ministry I found it easier to just pray over people rather than ask them what their needs were. I didn't want to know in case nothing happened. Great man of faith! I laid hands on the lady and prayed. She seemed content enough and went on her way.

"A few days later, the local undertaker saw me walking downtown and yelled, 'Hey Rev. Did you know what happened to so and so (referring to this teacher)?' No, I didn't, I confessed. 'Well, she was blind in one eye but now she can see!'

"It began a revival in this small town. The church filled every Sunday. People getting saved and baptized in the Holy Spirit. Folks getting healed, including a gang leader whose abscessed teeth were instantly healed. He came back the next day to learn more about this Jesus and found Christ. He went back to his clan and led many to Christ.

"It all started and continued with praise. Praise opened our hearts to His presence and His presence brought all the benefits of the Kingdom of God.

"10 years later I was driving a taxi. Those memories seemed distant until someone recognized me at a Greyhound station. This person, as if a gift from the Lord, reminded me of my time there saying, 'You need to get back into ministry – you shook up a whole town.'

"Fortunately, I did."

5. **Be in a position of prayer.**

Increase your life of contemplation – possibly the other end of the spectrum to public praise and worship, but so critical to learning the voice of the Lord. By "contemplation," with apologies to the experts on the classic spiritual disciplines, especially J. Richard Foster and Dallas Willard, I'm referring to that quiet time before God that we should yearn for every day.

If you're too busy for this – you're too busy.

The great R.A. Torrey once said:

> "We are too busy to pray, and so we are too busy to have power."[3]

Preferably at the start of each day, read the Word, pray the Word, talk to God, but also LISTEN to God.

It may be an illustration of the scriptures you've just read, or He will place on your mind someone or something for which to intercede. Or, maybe it will be a powerful word about you that heals a portion of your soul. Either one, it is God himself, through the Holy Spirit, speaking directly to your spirit an intimate secret, an intimate revelation that will draw you closer to Him.

"Prayer is not monologue, but dialogue. God's voice in response to mine is its most essential part."[4] – Andrew Murray

My point being, listening is active. If you don't expect God to speak then your time of

If you don't expect God to speak then your time of contemplation will be dry.

contemplation will be dry. And this learning to listen will teach you to trust what you are hearing. When God speaks to you an intimate secret about somebody else (a word of knowledge) you'll be more prepared to share it. And practice listening to the Spirit outside your prayer closet and in day-to-day life.

1 Kings 19:10-13 is the story of Elijah in the cave, complaining to the Lord that people are out to kill him, "I have been very zealous for you, Lord…"

Carefully read the Lord's reply in words and deed:

> *Then He said, "Go out, and stand on the mountain before the Lord." And behold, the Lord passed by, and a great and strong wind tore into the mountains and broke the rocks in pieces before the Lord, but the Lord was not in the wind; and after the wind an*

earthquake, but the Lord was not in the
earthquake; and after the earthquake a
fire, but the Lord was not in the fire; and after the fire a
still small voice.

A still small voice – after all the dramatics, the Lord spoke to Elijah through a still small voice. Of course, being in the cave he was in a good position to listen!

<u>Here's the key:</u> Putting yourself in a position to hear from God – a lot depends on the question you ask and what you are listening for. Daily, even several times a day, ask the Lord, "What are you doing? What are you saying, Lord?"

6. **Be in a position of asking.**

    After all is said and done about receiving the gifts of the Holy Spirit and about receiving the baptism of the Holy Spirit, it involves asking.

    Ask.

    In my ministry I've participated in over 100,000 people, of every age group and multiple ethnicities, receiving the fullness of the Spirit. Probably one of the main reasons I've been blessed to see so much fruit in this area is that I keep it simple and stay in the Scriptures.

    These are the scriptures I quote:

Ask, and it will be given to you; seek, and you will find; knock, and it will be opened to you. For everyone who asks receives, and he who seeks finds, and to him who knocks it will be opened. Or what man is there among you who, if his son asks for bread, will give him a stone? Or if he asks for a fish, will he give him a serpent? If you then, being evil, know how to give good gifts to your children, how much more will your Father who is in heaven give good things to those who ask Him! Matthew 7:7-11

In Luke 11:11-13, Jesus says it this way:

If a son asks for bread from any father among you, will he give him a stone? Or if he asks for a fish, will he give him a serpent instead of a fish? Or if he asks for an egg, will he offer him a scorpion? If you then, being evil, know how to give good gifts to your children, how much more will your heavenly Father give the Holy Spirit to those who ask Him!"

Do you want everything, every good gift from above? Of course you do.

If you believe God is good and believe in the words of Jesus, ask Him and He will give you good gifts; He will give you the Holy Spirit to fill you. This is an absolute promise. This is the will of God for you, for everyone.

Do you want everything, every good gift from above? Of course you do.

So ask and then receive.

A dear friend, who had been a successful businessman, felt the call of God to give up the business life and go into the ministry. He began the process by enrolling in LIFE Bible College and pressing through until graduation. I was there to pray with him when he was licensed and released to do the work of the Lord.

He quickly took a role at a local church as a staff pastor but kept telling me over and over that his real desire was to preach and to be a senior pastor. Then one day came a big opportunity for him to speak in a good established church. It was his first time preaching and he was terrified. Very nervous about speaking his first time to a larger congregation, he asked me, "What should I do?"

I told him, if you really want a move of God, invite the Holy Spirit to take over and then watch what happens. Simply ask Him to come. My friend listened and I was there to witness the power of thc Spirit wash over a congregation. People were healed, set free, and delivered when my friend simply invited the Holy Spirit to do as He would desire. The service ended up going for hours with people crying and calling out to God for His touch. This was the catalyst event that propelled my friend to planting his own church and leading a thriving congregation to this day.

7. Be in a position of waiting.

Acts 1:8 has an underlying tension – a tension we've probably all experienced. Those disciples, only weeks before, were emotionally crushed. All their hope and dreams vanished with the crucifixion. Now the risen Jesus had given them hopeful final words before He rose into the clouds, "You shall receive power …" Yet, they didn't know when this divine exchange would occur. So all they could do was wait. Waiting on the Holy Spirit… in our culture is difficult, to say the least. We want, we demand, instant gratification. Much of what Jesus said remained foreign to the disciples until the Spirit brought understanding.

Intuitively, and through Jesus' words, they understood that this power was different and new. He had forbidden them to use things which people consider powerful – persuasive speech, personal charisma, intellectual dominance. Instead, they would have divine power to proclaim the Kingdom, and signs and wonders would follow.

Let the words of the great preacher and writer G. Campbell Morgan stir you:

> "They (the disciples) have no sword save the sword of the Spirit... I see a group of men who do not impress their age by what they are in themselves. Remember this, the one thing that puzzled, supremely puzzled, priests and Pharisees and rulers was how these men did these things. How do you account for it? And I hear their own answers, 'We are witnesses of these things; and so is the Holy Ghost.' That is the answer."[5]

Unlike the first disciples waiting for the Spirit to come, we have the fullness of the Spirit to rely upon. Yet there is a principle for Spirit led believers to glean in Acts 2.

a. They were committed to waiting on the Lord before doing ministry. These disciples had previously been sent out by Jesus and had seen signs and wonders follow; yet they chose to wait, as they were instructed.

b. They were in "one accord." The Greek word indicates being in agreement with one mind and purpose. They weren't haphazardly waiting – like waiting by a pool or hanging out. These men were

serious and they sought the Lord. Knowing that
your beliefs may end up costing you your life can be
sobering.

Waiting and witnessing go hand in hand. Of course,
opportunities to share your faith may happen spontaneously.
However, as a church and even as an individual, spend time
"actively" waiting on the Lord to see where He will lead you to
"be a witness."

There are groups, often of
young people, who first pray
and seek the Lord for who they
will witness to, eventually
seeing in the Spirit vivid
descriptions of an individual
that needs Christ. It's not the
only way to witness, but it is
one that teaches us dependence
upon the Spirit – and that's a
good thing!

> The Gifts flow
> from believers
> who are full of
> the Spirit and
> are in a
> constant state
> of waiting on
> the Spirit.

Moving in the Gifts involves waiting on the Spirit. The Gifts
are not yours to possess and act upon at your will. The Gifts
flow from believers who are full of the Spirit and are in a
constant state of waiting on the Spirit – in a way modeled

by Jesus.

> *Very truly I tell you, the Son can do nothing by himself;*
> *he can do only which he sees his Father doing, because*
> *whatever the Father does the Son also does.* **John 5:19**

In my years of pastoring and mission work, it has been clear to me that I can move in the "flow" of the Spirit. It's a state or place where I find myself more about my Father's business than my own. There are seasons, probably due to our flesh, when this "flow" is more powerful and evident.

The Bible calls us "vessels," and out of vessels flow that which the vessel is filled with. We are poured out until we are empty. Yet, we, like the first disciples, know there will be a fresh infilling for our life. Hopefully our lives are a continual filling, then flowing, and then filling again – because we were never created to operate on our own in our own strength.

> *"Not by might nor by power, but by My Spirit," says the*
> LORD *of hosts.* **Zechariah 4:6**

I love the story that John Wimber was fond of telling about the beginning of the Vineyard Church movement. Once the Lord spoke to him about stepping out in healing, so he devoted an entire year to teaching on the subject – 55 straight weeks on healing. The result? Nobody was healed, some got worse, and John even caught a few of their sicknesses. Yet, they waited on the Lord and eventually, as John would express it, "God showed up."

The lesson that stayed with Wimber and other Vineyard leaders, "Wait on the Lord." Don't be pressed to act or move until you hear the voice of the Lord.

But then once you hear it, step out in faith.

8. **Be in a position to receive or give an impartation.**

    <u>Ananias and Paul</u>

    > *Now there was a certain disciple at Damascus named Ananias; and to him the Lord said in a vision, "Ananias."*
    >
    > *And he said, "Here I am, Lord."*
    >
    > *So the Lord said to him, "Arise and go to the street called Straight, and inquire at the house of Judas for one called Saul of Tarsus, for behold, he is praying. And in a vision he has seen a man named Ananias coming in and putting his hand on him, so that he might receive his sight.* Acts 9:10-12

    Can you imagine the immediate emotions surging through Ananias' mind after receiving a vision from the Lord? First, the vision itself – we too often read the Bible as if everyone in it was a sea-parting saint, seeing multiple visions from God.

But Ananias recovered quickly to reply to the Lord:

> *Lord, I have heard from many about this man, how much harm he has done to your saints in Jerusalem.* Acts 9:13

You have to wonder if Ananias, on the way to Straight Street to the house of Judas to see Saul, questioned his sanity for questioning the Lord. Something along the lines of, in the Greek, "Well duh, Ananias. You get your one and only direct encounter with God, and you question His wisdom!"

Nevertheless, this disciple at Damascus obeyed God.

> *And Ananias went his way and entered the house: and laying his hands on him he said, "Brother Saul, the Lord Jesus, who appeared to you on the road as you came, has sent me that you may receive your sight and be filled with the Holy Spirit." Immediately then fell from his eyes something like scales, and he received his sight at once; and he arose and was baptized.* Acts 9:17-18

The Laying On of Hands

    a.   Without question, the laying on of hands as a means of imparting the Holy Spirit is a biblical reality.

In Acts alone there are five accounts when people receive the baptism in the Holy Spirit – in three cases those seeking the baptism were ministered to by believers' laying on of hands. In the Upper Room in Jerusalem and in Cornelius' home, people received the baptism directly.

b. Everyone is invited to "lay on hands." It is not restricted to the holders of ecclesiastical office. Ananias is described simply as a disciple. Jesus himself said:

> *And these signs will follow those who believe: In my name they will... speak with new tongues... they will lay hands on the sick, and they will recover.* **Mark 16:17-18**

He clearly did not confine the laying on of hands to a special class of believer – we all can lay hands on one another for the purpose of imparting the Holy Spirit.

Yet, this practice is not to be exercised lightly. Paul exhorts Timothy:

> *Do not lay hands on anyone hastily, nor share in other people's sins, keep yourself pure.*
> **1 Timothy 5:22**

c. The other purpose of the laying on of hands is the imparting of spiritual gifts.

Paul said to Timothy:

> *Do not neglect the gift that is in you, which was given to you by prophecy with the laying on of the hands of the eldership.* 1 Timothy 4:14

One of the greatest joys in my life was having Evelyn Thompson lay hands on me and pray for a fresh anointing of the Spirit. She had received a similar blessing from Sister Aimee Semple McPherson as a LIFE Bible College student. Sister Thompson, as she was affectionately referred to, went on to lead an extraordinary life as an evangelist and functioned in all the Gifts.

I'll never forget an experience in 110 degree heat in Phoenix, Arizona a few years ago during our denomination's convention. I was walking across the street with my dearest friend from Indonesia, Dr. Andre Hanney Mandey. During Dr. Mandey's time as president, the movement grew from 2,500 to over 18,000 churches in the largest Muslim nation in the world.

Another pastor, recognizing this apostolic leader, on the blazing hot pavement in the middle of the crosswalk, got on his knees and asked Dr. Mandey for a blessing. Dr. Mandey prayed for him while I worried about oncoming traffic. This incident always reminds me of the issue of desire – how much do we want the blessings, the gifts of God?

Is there an Ananias in your life or are you an Ananias to others?

Are we willing to go to those Jesus is sending us to, those we may fear or hate, and be obedient to impart a life-transforming experience?

Ananias laid hands on arguably the greatest apostle of all, Paul, who opened up the Gentile world to the gospel; but he had to overcome his prejudices and fears before he would obey God.

Are we willing to go to those Jesus is sending us to, those we may fear or hate, and be obedient to impart a life-transforming experience?

Ananias simultaneously imparted the gift of the Holy Spirit, yet willingly stepped out of the way and out of the spotlight – you never hear about him again. This led to a transfer of power and ultimately to the healing of the Church. Are we willing to get out of the way for the Kingdom's sake?

A.J. Swoboda concluded a powerful message at a recent convention stating plainly:

> "Every single person in the room is a result of some Ananias laying hands on you."[6]

Impartation of the Gifts is the imparting not only of the Spirit, but of your life to another.

Impartation of the Gifts is the imparting not only of the Spirit, but of your life to another. It may be a one-time obedient act like Ananias to Saul, or it may be a point in time of a committed mentorship. Either way, it's something we all can participate in.

Some may receive more attention and spotlight than others, but we all share in the joy of seeing the fruit of the Kingdom established.

Impartation Checklist

I'm kind of a freak when it comes to checklists for things that must be accomplished, so bear with me:

- Has anyone laid hands on you to either receive the Holy Spirit or to receive the gifts of the Spirit?

- Are you open to receiving the Gifts? Are you open to praying for others to receive?

- Who is the Ananias in your life? Who are you an Ananias to?

- Why do you desire the spiritual Gifts? Have you asked the Holy Spirit to reveal to you your true motives?

- Are you willing to use the Gifts to further God's Kingdom on earth?

- Are you willing to see the Gifts imparted to those outside your comfort zone, even those you may fear?

- Are you willing to receive from someone outside your "tribe"?

- Are you open to being patient, seeking the Gifts even after not receiving?

And probably the most important thing is, according to Pastor Tony Krishack of Houston, Texas, "Are you desperate for more of God? Those who are desperate to receive a touch from God — receive a touch from God. And those not desperate will often find fault with those He touches."

Given by the Spirit

The Word of WISDOM

REQUEST it

DIVINE UNDERSTANDING

"truth bomb"

TRUTH

BEYOND Human Wisdom

UNLOCK HURT & SHAME

I Cor. 12:8

A GIFT from the LORD

Chapter Six

Living the Revelation Gifts:
Get Wisdom

The Word of Wisdom

It's one of the most sobering, yet humorous stories regarding things of the Spirit I've ever heard, though it came to me third hand.

My brother-in-law used to meet at 6:00 a.m. every morning for prayer with an old saint affectionately referred to as "Papa Jones." By 6:00 a.m. this man of God had already spent two hours in the presence of the Lord. Rev. Jones used to occasionally minister in the same circles as Smith Wigglesworth and John G. Lake, giants of the faith.

One day, as the story goes, all three, along with many other substantial leaders, gathered together for prayer. As one could expect, the room filled with faith and expectation. Prayers and the prophetic moved seamlessly throughout the large room. As was the custom of the day, many prophetic utterances began with a declarative and distinctly Old Testament, "Thus saith the Lord." Wigglesworth, Lake, et al gave words that shook the room!

Then Papa Jones, a young man learning to move in the Gifts with the big boys, began to loudly prophesy, "Thus saith the Lord God of Israel!" The rest of the message, as he recalled, sounded like many others he had heard. But the young Jones knew as he spoke that which started in the Spirit had rapidly moved to the flesh. He had the wisdom and discernment to know the difference.

Most of us would have concluded our "message" and sheepishly sat down, but not Papa Jones. The fear of the Lord moved as powerfully as the Gifts in those days. There would be no hiding. Young Jones, with the same powerful but youthful voice, declared mid-sentence to the entire room, after the briefest of pause, "Flesh, Flesh, Flesh!" And then he sat down.

I don't know the rest of the story. Did John G. or Smith console the young man afterward? But I do know that Rev. Jones lived a full life of faith, no doubt always fearing the Lord, not man.

As we look at and move in each of the nine gifts, may we all walk in that fear and humility as did dear Brother Jones.

Pentecostal scholar Dr. Donald Gee writes:

"All the 'treasures of wisdom and knowledge' are hid in Christ (Colossians 2:3). Severed from His grace a counsel of utter foolishness can be given even by one who at other times has had truly supernatural flashes of the spiritual gift. Its manifestation is subject to divine sovereignty, and dependent upon the Spirit-filled believer walking in unbroken communion with the Lord."[1]

> We all can move between the flesh and the Spirit, even in an instant.

In other, less eloquent, words: Be careful when giving or receiving a "word of wisdom" or any prophetic gift. We all can move between the flesh and the Spirit, even in an instant. Acknowledging this truth keeps us humble and continually seeking his grace.

Definition:

Former missionary and friend of Smith Wigglesworth, Howard Carter, in his book *Questions and Answers on Spiritual Gifts* gives one of the best, succinct definitions of the word of wisdom:

"The word of wisdom might be defined as a supernatural revelation of the mind and purpose of God communicated by the Holy Spirit. It is God's wisdom imparted to man... When the Lord specifically reveals His purpose to an individual, that person possesses a word of God's wisdom."[2]

Carter further and rightfully notes:

"Quite apart from this supernatural gift of the Holy Spirit, however, the Lord is willing to guide believers in their daily affairs, and to give them wisdom, as required for any particular circumstances, in the same way as He is willing to heal the sick apart from the gifts of healing."[3]

Wisdom is the Thing

God values wisdom. The Bible is replete with teaching on wisdom's importance in our lives.

Proverbs 4:7 reminds us:

> *Wisdom is the principal thing; therefore get wisdom.*
> *And in all your getting, get understanding.*

I love it... it almost has a "street" vibe to it. But it's true. Without wisdom, all the gifts – natural and supernatural – have the potential for shipwreck.

How many times have you seen it? Someone in the church who seems full of the Holy Ghost, but doesn't possess the wisdom to apply their gifting.

Or, the person who knows every Greek irregular verb, but lacks understanding of the Scripture for everyday application.

Worst of all, the learned, gifted, even charismatic individual who ends up in a cult-like fanaticism because of a lack of wisdom.

Then, there's just plain dumb.

He was the most charismatic individual I'd ever met. He prayed in tongues, cast out demons, and seemingly had a word of prophecy for everyone.

Though I was young in the things of the Spirit at the time, I had maturity in the Word and a keen perception of people. I knew, even then, spiritually gifted people did not mean they were always wise or without occasional poor motivations. Gifted people make mistakes, even when exercising the Gifts. Though it bothered me then, and it bothers me today, I only have to find a mirror to reflect on my shared human failings and adjust my judgmentalism.

This brother, however, tested my young, forgiving heart. Though he had an obvious weight problem, I'd never heard him address it, until one day, out of the blue, as we drove into a fast food restaurant, he stated boldly, "I'm on the Holy Spirit Diet!" He paused and I waited for the punch line. "I just pray over anything I eat and the Holy Spirit will take care of the calories." I waited some more, hoping with every fiber he would burst out in the same laughter welling up inside me. But he was very serious.

Being an older brother in the Lord, and due to our mentoring relationship, I remained quiet. But the experience has never left my memory because it reminds me that wisdom must always come when moving in the Gifts. Yet, the gift of wisdom is seen as distinct from the general wisdom mentioned in Proverbs 4:7.

Good Question

Did Paul, through the unction of the Spirit, put the word of wisdom first in line of the nine Gifts for a similar reason? Possibly... although the wisdom in Proverbs is God-given and we are told to seek it; and Paul, in Colossians, prayed for it (Colossians 1:9). The word of wisdom seems to be of a special level – a supernatural level – dispensed by the Spirit as with the other eight Gifts. (Otherwise, why would it be listed in that grouping?)

In fact Paul, in the chapters leading up to Chapter 12, discusses wisdom and how he deliberately put aside natural wisdom (and if anyone possessed natural wisdom, it was Paul) so that he could be filled with a supernatural wisdom of the Spirit (1 Corinthians 2:1-4).

The church today, individuals today, must contend for spiritual wisdom over natural wisdom when seeking to do the will of the Lord. Buy that building? Marry that person? Natural wisdom will take you so far, but the ultimate answer must come from God.

Dr. Gee states it insightfully well:

"In a manifestation of the spiritual gift of the word of wisdom, something flashes. There is a sense of the divine, a consciousness of an utterance transcending human experience. One is deeply conscious that the supremely right thing has been said and the true course of action indicated."[4]

He goes on to confidently say:

"No further appeal is desired because the heart rests in a calm satisfaction that the will of God has been revealed."

I've experienced that in a meeting of elders or even with my

It can change the direction of your life. It can provide a pathway forward when you feel hopelessly stuck.

wife over dinner. We'll pause and look at each other, knowing God just spoke. But the common denominator is you know that these words of wisdom came from outside your own wisdom and understanding, even the spiritual, scriptural kind.

It can change the direction of your life. It can provide a pathway forward when you feel hopelessly stuck. And it can come from multiple sources.

The Purpose(s) of the Word of Wisdom

Here are a few of the purposes or effects of the word of wisdom (with much insight from David Pytches, *Spiritual Gifts in the Local Church*[5]) – not in any order of significance or frequency:

1. Help the church body or individual determine what is best to do in a situation

2. Help to apply the insights that are revealed through a word of knowledge or prophecy, etc.

    *   How to pray for a person especially when praying for healing or demonic deliverance

    *   How to reveal a difficult insight revealed through a word of knowledge

3. Help the church or individual avoid a danger or a negative situation in the future

4. Help the church or individual with understanding of a revelation of the future

   • Discerning God's plan for an upcoming event - For example, the Lord gives a revelation of His purpose, such as the destruction of Sodom and Gomorrah

New York, New York

On an ordinary Sunday in September, the keyboard player at our church, and a very good friend who flew often because of his job, came to me in a panic. Sweat literally running down his face, shaking he said, "Pastor, please pray for me." I asked him what was wrong. He replied, "I don't know what is wrong, but the Lord is telling me not to get on a plane tonight to go to New York City." I responded matter of factly, "Well, don't go."

"But I have to, it's my job," he said.

We talked for a while; but he, despite the warning from God and my advice to heed that warning, took the flight to New York City, mainly because his wife had told him, "Just go to work."

While in New York City, he and fellow co-workers were given some unexpected free time, so my friend, the keyboard player, said, "Hey, let's be the first ones this morning to go up into the World Trade Center."

It was Tuesday morning, September 11, 2001.

Just as they were about to go up the tower, his phone rang. His boss ordered them to immediately leave and head to Boston. As they drove away in their car, the first plane hit the tower.

He called me while I was at the church watching the tragedy of 9/11 unfold. "I was just there. I was just there!" he excitedly repeated. "This is what the Lord was telling me."

I told him how we as a church the night before had prayed fervently for him. The church truly contended for his safety. Can you imagine how his wife would have felt if he'd stayed just a few minutes longer?

He had a word of knowledge and was given a word of wisdom, but he chose to ignore both. Despite that, the Lord showed him mercy. The Lord will give you wisdom for the future. Be obedient and listen.

Banda Aceh, Indonesia

The day after Christmas 2004, a giant tsunami hit killing over 200,000 people – one of the greatest natural disasters ever. Because this was a region of the world I oversaw for Foursquare Missions, I immediately flew to this disaster site.

After arriving, one of my first questions to the local leaders was, "How many people did we lose?"

The answer stunned me. In fact, I thought they misunderstood my question.

"What do you mean we didn't lose anybody?"

"None of our pastors or church members died."

Then they began to share how that could happen when we had plenty of churches within the disaster area.

"Several of the pastors and others felt from the Lord to celebrate Christmas up in the mountains... so all the believers left."

One after another shared how they had felt from the Lord to go up into the mountains. They all obeyed and were all protected.

Fiesta in Mexico

The day had arrived – Christmas in the little town of Cerro Azul, just outside Tecate, Mexico. My church had previously built a large church and a few homes in this town of hard-working, but dirt-poor families.

This pueblo of about 500 people had become second home to many of us, so celebrating Christmas came naturally. Our church, knowing each and every family, bought gifts for them all, including the many children. We also bought food and drinks to have a proper Christmas party. Everything was set to celebrate. We expected to have a wonderful time – American and Mexican families, each who had learned to love and learn from each other.

Then the buses began to come. As the leader of the event, I asked why. The answer stunned me – first, because I should have anticipated it, and second, I did not know what to do.

The word had gotten out about our party. Hundreds began to pour in. I estimated our approximate 500 people ballooned to 1,500. All I could think about were the sad faces of adults and children when I announced the party would be cancelled because it was too late to turn the buses back. To this day, I know that the only thing that stopped me from cancelling was a word of wisdom.

As I spoke to my worried leaders and dozens of Mexican cooks, I was reminded of the feeding of the 5,000 and the 4,000.

"If it happened then, it can happen now," I said with as much faith as I could muster. And then I emphatically added, "Pray!"

All I know, and anyone who was there will tell you, is that at the end of the day, everyone was fed and everyone got a gift –

everyone. Not one sad face or disappointed word, but a lot of relieved and rejoicing leaders and cooks!

Jesus Operating in a Word of Wisdom

Jesus, according to Philippians 2:6-8, willingly laid down His divinity to become the likeness of man. In so doing, He operated within the confines of his humanity, moving, as we do, in the gifts of the Spirit.

In John 4:16-18, Jesus encounters the Samaritan woman. He has a word of knowledge of this woman's five previous husbands; but in a word of wisdom, He gently tells her to "go, call your husband, and come here." It was the Father's gracious way, through Jesus, of confronting her.

- In a similar manner, Jesus gently confronts the rich, young ruler. In Mark 10:17-22, Jesus answers the rich ruler's question about eternal life. His motivation in this conversation was love (verse 21) and his supernatural wisdom went to the heart of this young man's personal issue without humiliating him.

- It was wisdom that had Jesus prepare for a miracle in John 2:7 when He had the servants fill the wine pots with water.

- In the feeding of both the 5,000 and the 4,000, Jesus displays a supernatural wisdom by having the crowds sit and tell the disciples to gather what they could (Mark 6:30-43, Mark 8:1-9). The actual miracle came after the meager provisions arrived.

- Jesus' word of wisdom was on display when enemies tried to trap or criticize Him. The most famous being a reply that even the most hardened secularists admire today. When confronted with the adulterous woman, He, seeing their own hearts, says, "He who is without sin among you, cast the first stone." (John 8:7)[6]

Another test that left them "marveling" is found in Matthew 22:21,

> *Render therefore to Caesar the things that are Caesar's and to God the things that are God's.*

Wisdom at Joppa

In Acts 10, Peter has the vision of a sheet filled with unclean animals that will ultimately lead to the first outreach to the Gentile world.

Peter hears a voice in verse 15:

> *What God has cleansed you must not call common.*

Between the time of the voice and his encounter with Cornelius, supernatural wisdom gave Peter full understanding of his vision:

> *But God has shown me that I should not call any man common or unclean.* (verse 28)

Peter did not have to guess or surmise what the vision meant, the Holy Spirit told him.

The word of wisdom may take us to places we least expect or want to go, but the results will always be to His glory.

He would begin his sermon to Cornelius' household, a Gentile household – formerly forbidden to enter and unclean to a Jew:

> *In truth I perceive that God shows no partiality.* (verse 34)

While still speaking, the "Holy Spirit fell upon all those who heard the word" (verse 44) and they all spoke with tongues.

Peter was given supernatural wisdom not only to understand the vision, but wisdom to go into an "unclean" home and preach the gospel. The word of wisdom may take us to places we least expect or want to go, but the results will always be to His glory.

Randy Clark sums up word of wisdom best:

"A Word of Wisdom, then, refers to a supernatural wisdom given in the moment that leads a person to make the right decision, or reply with the right answer, or break through an impasse, or know what to do in a particular situation. It is a wisdom that has nothing to do with IQ and is not gained by human experience or learning, but is supernaturally given by God."[7]

I believe the Holy Spirit gave a son supernatural wisdom to honor his failing father one last time in the following story:

"Had to place my father in dementia care today and drive away. I can only be there every couple of weeks so I taped this to his door. I want the staff to know who the new man in #14 truly is."

My name is Bill Mead.

I was born in abject poverty.

I became a warrior (US Navy, Korean War era).

I then laid aside my weapons and

Became a minister and missionary.

I traveled the world, spreading the

Gospel of Jesus Christ,

Bringing hope, medicine, and love

To the United States, Europe,

South America, and Africa.

I am slowly leaving this earth

For my heavenly home.

This may take awhile.

Thank you for remembering who I was

And who I am.

I am a man, a warrior, a missionary,

A father, a friend, and much more.

And I have one more river to cross.[8]

SUPERNATURAL *Revelation*

The **WORD** of

THE STILL SMALL **VOICE**

KNOWLEDGE

CAUTION: *MOVE in Humility*

SETTING CAPTIVES FREE

LISTEN
to the Spirit

RISK

read your mail

SPEAK <u>ONLY IN</u> LOVE

Chapter Seven

Living the Revelation Gifts: Knowing the Unknowable

The Word of Knowledge

With the sun casting no shadow, the woman walked, holding her empty jar tightly to her side, toward the ancient well. This time of day usually gave her invisibility, but she noticed a man slumped against its stones, someone she did not recognize.

As custom demanded, no look or words to this stranger. But she spotted His distinctive shawl protecting His head from the sun. He was a Jew. It made the next moment extraordinary.

As she leaned her water jar against the well, called Jacob's Well to all who knew the old story, she proceeded to grab the rope to lower her jar.

The stranger spoke, startling her, "Give me a drink."

His request, which normally would have received a rebuke from this woman unafraid of any man, was given in a tone that was neither demanding nor passive. His voice intrigued her, causing her to defy both cultural and religious prohibitions to engage Him.

"How is it that you, being a Jew, ask a drink of me, a Samaritan woman?" Looking for His reaction, she continued before He could speak, stating the obvious, "For Jews have no dealing with Samaritans."

But it is hard to consider heaven when the heat draws water from your pores like the jar draws from the well.

His response ignored her attempt at argument, preferring to take the conversation to a deeper plane, speaking about living water. Maybe she was confused, probably sarcastic, "Where then do you get that living water?" She didn't wait for the answer, but doubled up on the stranger. If sarcasm wasn't enough, maybe a who-do-you-think-you-are question, "Are you greater than our father, Jacob?"

Again, the stranger didn't bite; He wanted the conversation not to be political, but personal. Her response indicated He was beginning to reach this woman whose mind must have been racing between the temporal and eternal. But it is hard to consider heaven when the heat draws water from your pores like the jar draws from the well.

The stranger, sensing a breakthrough, told her to go, call her husband, and then return; for He knew something only revealed to Him from above. Her reply was to the point, but not completely forthcoming, "I have no husband."

The stranger, armed with supernatural knowledge of this woman, began with a compliment quickly followed by a harsh, but liberating, truth. She had failed five times in marriage and was now living in sin. Her "failure" most probably resulted from rejection by the five men, possibly because she was barren. She lived with that and the cultural stain of being unclean. But He perceived her heart and His words would ultimately bring her freedom.

The layers of her hard life were being peeled back and though she fought to protect herself with one more religious argument, the stranger's words brought her rare hope. Her final reply, no longer to argue, but in some way she wanted to connect with this man who must be a prophet, "I know the Messiah is coming. When He comes, He will tell us all things."

She didn't notice that the stranger's friends had returned when He said something that she would tell her community over and over again in the days to come. Their eyes locked in a moment of pure revelation, "I who speak to you am He."

She would leave her water pot, while the disciples worried about food, and begin a mission to her people, the Samaritans. Many believed after her testimony of the encounter and the words this stranger, Jesus, spoke to them. Not a bad strategy: testimony and then the Word – living water for all.

The word of knowledge Jesus had concerning her past and current marital status, along with words of wisdom and revelation, obviously played a big part in her conversion and then mission. It cut through all her arguments and doubt. As disciples of this same Jesus, we too are given this gift – not for ourselves, but to help unlock "the mystery which has been hidden for ages" to another.

Setting Captives Free

The moment Ray poked his head into my office I knew everything – the whats, the whys, the hows. He didn't have any idea what God was about to do.

No one I had ever met before had been under such demonic bondage: drugs, alcohol, witchcraft. In fact, witchcraft had been passed down to him from many generations. When Ray first came to me he was desperate. I didn't know it at the time, but I believe God gave me the gift of the word of wisdom as I instructed him to spend three days with no T.V. and radio, and fast and pray before I would pray for him.

As soon as I laid hands on him, the freedom came and the chains of bondage broke. Completely transformed, he sang in the choir, read the Word faithfully, and experienced the healing of many relationships. Now he stood at the door of my office, and without a word, I knew why. The bondages were knocking on his door.

"Ray, before you tell me anything, let me tell you why you're here," I told him immediately as he sat down.

His eyes got big and I continued. "The reason you're here is that a lot of demonic strongholds are trying to get back into your life." I got a little more specific. I had his attention. "They are not in you but surrounding you, to bring you back into bondage."

Ray was both stunned at my revelation and relieved at the same time. Then I had one last word that confirmed to him that the God who had originally set him free still loved

God wants to use you to speak into the lives of those who need to know God cares.

him and wanted nothing to harm their relationship. "You've started to smoke again, haven't you, Ray?"

"How did you know?" Even as he asked the question, he knew the answer. God was revealing all truth to set him free once more. I explained that the enemy of his soul was using a former bondage (smoking) as a kind of trigger point to flood him with his past.

A word of knowledge and wisdom – a gift given not for personal blessing, but to set captives free. As with the woman at the well, God wants to use you to speak into the lives of those who need to know God cares. He does. Even about the most personal things in life.

A Very Personal Word

As hackneyed as this phrase is it aptly describes the moment, *she took my breath away.* Before my 20-year-old self stood the most stunning woman I had ever met. And the fact that she was at church and probably a Christian... life couldn't get much better.

Fortunately, words came out of my mouth, although they were a little too serious for my liking. "What are you doing with your life?" To my relief, she didn't laugh and walk away.

We spoke briefly when she offered some rather intimate insight, especially to someone she had just met.

"I'm going to marry a minister," she said almost matter-of-factly, not knowing that I was a youth pastor wanting to give my life to full-time ministry. Bells, whistles, angels descending from heaven – it was the Fourth of July fireworks exploding in my mind.

But there is more to this story.

She was raised in a devout Catholic family. As a young teenager, after a tragic event in her life, she stayed with her grandparents during recovery. Her grandmother decided to take her to the church's Tuesday evening prayer service for the sick. At the invitation for prayer, her grandmother pulled her from the pew to the front of the church.

A layman prayed over my future bride. She experienced heat go through her body with the hand of God pressing on her lungs, while seeing bright flashes of light with both eyes closed. As she opened her eyes she proclaimed, "Jesus is real and He loves me," and she was instantly healed, born again, and baptized in the Holy Spirit with speaking in tongues.

Everything now revolved around the church. As a young girl, she had an incredibly vivid encounter with God and He spoke to her, "You are going to marry a minister. I've got someone prepared for you."

Because of her Catholic background, this was extremely confusing. A minister was a priest. Priests don't marry. Yet, she never deviated from this word, hiding it in her heart until she met me, a young college student.

Absolutely on fire for God, she began to attend prayer meetings, Bible studies, and revival nights. She even carried her extra large, hard cover King James Bible everywhere, including to her high school.

> It is not given just to disseminate knowledge or prove one's spirituality, but is given to produce fruit, like the woman at the well.

At age 20, a friend invited her to a college/career group at a church where I interned as a youth pastor. That's where I blurted out my first words to her. Four months later we were married.

What is a Word of Knowledge?

It is a supernatural revelation of knowledge, not acquired through natural means. Usually it is a fragment of information given by God for a person or a situation. It is truth that the

Holy Spirit wants revealed to produce a desired result.

It is not given just to disseminate knowledge or prove one's spirituality, but is given to produce fruit, like the woman at the well. She was not one who easily believed. In fact, she argued repeatedly at the well with the very Son of God! Jesus' word of knowledge helped to cut away the hardness surrounding her heart.

Sometimes it's given to protect the flock – insights into someone who might bring harm to others. Other times it may be knowledge that serves as a warning – the classic story being John Wimber sitting next to a complete stranger on a 747 jet. God revealed to him supernatural knowledge regarding the stranger's adulterous affair, even the name of the woman, including a warning that unless he repented, God would soon take his life. The man not only repented and received Christ, but also confessed to his wife while on the plane, even leading her to Jesus.[1]

There are times knowledge is dropped into our hearts and minds from the Spirit, which is for us personally. Yet still, it almost always has Kingdom ramifications – my wife's word regarding marrying a pastor, even when as a Catholic, she believed that to be impossible. However, our marriage has produced and continues to bear fruit globally for God. And, I am the first to declare it never would have happened without her in my life. In fact, she wouldn't have given me the time of day if she didn't have God's promise in her heart. Thank you, Jesus!

Simple Yet Profound

Sometimes a word of knowledge can be simple, yet potentially life changing.

While taking a small boat up and down the Amazon River to pray for people in various villages, its engine went out. Worse yet, it was in the middle of the widest part of the river and absolutely no one was around. No calling AAA for a tow. For over an hour we cranked the engine (it was a converted lawn mower engine!) to no avail except weary muscles and distraught hearts. We were a team of Americans full of "Go ye!" but little knowledge about machines.

This gift must be exercised with great caution and maturity. Humility must always be present in the operation of this gift as with others.

Finally someone, I think it was me, rather red-faced asked, "Did we pray over this engine?" After some strong intercession, we all looked at each other as the pull on the crank commenced.

Like new, the engine immediately started up and purred like a kitten.

A Supernatural Impartation

Like the other gifts, it is a supernatural impartation; its focus is a revelation of facts about someone or something. It's not knowledge discerned empirically or naturally. It can be a fragment of facts, an impression, or even an image.

Like the other gifts, it's not a permanent endowment. It comes as the Spirit wishes to reveal and bless. Even the revelation of sin (e.g., Jesus and the woman at the well) is meant to bring freedom from bondage, hence a blessing.

This gift must be exercised with great caution and maturity. Humility must always be present in the operation of this gift as with others.

Someone who moves powerfully in this gift, Mike Bickle, states it well:

"The Spirit conveys to our mind thoughts we imperfectly communicate with our words."[2]

Bickle's insight is most important and true for moving in all the Gifts. When frail, sinful man is trusted with a perfect gift, caution should always be taken. That's not to say we shouldn't be bold in stepping out in faith, but that we should always be humbly reflective by asking, "Did we hear correctly? Did we deliver properly?"

How Do We Move in this Gift?

Over the years of moving in this gift, I've developed a few principles:

1. **Learn to listen to "the still small voice" (1 Kings 19:11-12)**

   That voice is different for everyone. Some see images, feel impressions, even see words across a person's forehead. I've felt pain or sensations that I knew were not for me but for someone else. Sometimes it's an overwhelming emotion that would in the natural be very out of place.

   I've ministered to complete strangers when the Lord unexpectedly gave me an overwhelming love for them. It's an emotion reserved for your closest friends or family, yet God wants you to "feel it" so you can describe His love for the person to whom you are ministering. Usually once that love is expressed, further words or blessings follow.

2. **Always Be in the Position of Inquiring of the Lord**

   "Lord, what are you doing?" Then be willing to stop and listen. Don't be afraid of silence and waiting. It may come as a single word or impression, or in fact, you may not hear anything. Don't worry. It's in God's hands.

Again, Mike Bickle says it well:

> "God will not do our part and we cannot do his part."[3]

3. Be Willing to Step Out in Faith

You're open to the Spirit and the Lord gives you a single word or name. You can pray for more understanding and you can ask the person you are praying for, "Does this name mean something to you?" Be willing to take the time when ministering. You'll rarely get a complete Holy Spirit download all at once, especially when you first begin to move in the gift. "You are a former axe murderer with a tattoo of your mother on your left arm," probably won't happen, but then again, it can and does.

> Remember, your ability to discern between the Spirit and the flesh will continue to be refined as you continue to step out in faith.

Remember, your ability to discern between the Spirit and the flesh will continue to be refined as you continue to step out in faith.

4. **Stay Biblical and Stay Humble**

No word of knowledge will contradict or dishonor the Word of God.

> Be humble enough to say, "I think I got that wrong. Forgive me."

This is one of many reasons why every practitioner of the Gifts must be a student of the Word. If you don't know the Bible, you won't know that you've contradicted it. It is, of course, possible to have wrong images, words, sensations, etc. Usually when I say something that's off, the Spirit causes a real disquiet in my emotions. Be humble enough to say, "I think I got that wrong. Forgive me."

And by the way, not all words of knowledge you receive should be spoken. Ask God for wisdom.

5. **No Need to be Dramatic**

Although the gift can be emotional when received, we don't have to deliver it like we are an Old Testament prophet. I would normally suggest refraining from using opening phrases like, "Thus sayeth the Lord" or "The Lord told me." The more attention we call to ourselves, the less glory to God – not good. This kind of phrase raises the question, "Who can question the Lord?" I prefer, "I sense the Lord is saying..."

Plus, you don't have to deliver a word with the force of a stage actor. Actually, quiet and natural is preferred. Having said that, there are always exceptions. While ministering in other cultures, a low-key approach could be misunderstood. Again, the Gifts will work together, and a word of wisdom can precede a word of knowledge and impact how you deliver the word.

6. No Fear Allowed

One of the reasons so many believers fail to move consistently in this gift is that they are filled with the thought, "What if I miss it?" Guess what? You may. I remember a friend telling me that after giving a word to someone their reply was, "You're crazy!"

Personally, I probably would have taken my blanket and curled into a fetal position. Fortunately, my friend persevered and the Spirit gave further insight that brought healing.

It bears repeating, John Wimber's definition of moving in faith: R-I-S-K.

I remember, as a young pastor, interviewing someone for a position in the church. He was a family man and a member in good standing – nothing on the outside would indicate a problem.

But the Spirit shared intimate secrets about his past and present that disqualified him from this service. If I didn't know the Lord's voice, I never would have had the courage to confront him. Yet, because it was from God, this man expressed great relief that his secret life was exposed and he could begin a journey of healing.

7. **Reading "The Mail" is Not to Be Feared**

Fear can go both ways. Many times people will avoid someone they consider to be prophetic. Few people look forward to "having their mail read." This is often due to a misunderstanding of the gift. They view it primarily as a rebuke from God, an Ananias and Sapphira moment.

It's good to remember 1 Corinthians 12:7 –

But the manifestation of the Spirit is given to each one for the profit of all.

All of the gifts are meant to profit the body of Christ and they should not be feared. If you find your ministry is often confrontational or a delivery of secret knowledge – beware.

You thought this gift was "risky"? Just read the next…

Chapter Eight

Living the Revelation Gifts: Pick Your Spirits

Discerning of Spirits

She came like a ghost out from the rolling hills in the southern-most part of Tecate, Mexico – her beige gauze dress flowing in the slight breeze along with her long blonde hair.

Barefoot, the thin young woman glided into our encampment; both Americans and local Mexicans could only stare. A mixture of intrigue and anxiety grew as we could clearly see her albino skin pierced by jet black eyes.

Not knowing if she only spoke English or Spanish, my Mexican counterpart and I approached her. She spoke both fluently, but her voice did not fit her looks. A much older voice simultaneously enticed and repelled us.

Her conversation, along with the movements of her body, turned quickly to sexual perversion. Immediately we called out for the mature women elders of the village who firmly but lovingly took her away to minister to her.

Later we learned of the deep trauma this young woman had tragically experienced; but even the most seasoned women ministers could not free her from the bondage. Men were rightfully not allowed in the room or allowed to engage her. The spirits of seduction were strong. I've never encountered anything so powerful.

It is rare where such demonic manifestation is so clearly visible. Yet, the believer must be cognizant that severe trauma and mental disorder may not be demonic – we need the Holy Spirit to give us discernment, without which the process of healing will be severely compromised.

Spirit Beings

There exist in this universe three types of spirit beings. First is the human spirit. (1 Thessalonians 5:23) Body, soul, and spirit. We are all spirit beings, although most humans know little about this part of their essence. I find it interesting that some of the most primitive cultures are more aware of this spirit-self than so-called first world nations.

The second category is angelic spirits. Though similar to their human counterparts, there are unique differences. Angelic spirits divide into two main categories: demons and angels. The Scripture offers some, but sparse, insight into these unique beings.

> Simply, this gift allows the believer to distinguish the origin of the words and actions of an individual – are they from man, God, or Satan?

The third is the Spirit of God, also known as the Holy Spirit. Not that these categories are in any way equal, but each possesses a dimension that transcends the physical. And each is knowable by humans, especially when that human's spirit is regenerated by the Holy Spirit.

The gift of discerning of spirits involves a supernatural perception that allows an individual to perceive the type of spirit that is behind a person, especially their words and actions.

Simply, this gift allows the believer to distinguish the origin of the words and actions of an individual – are they from man, God, or Satan?

Like most of the Gifts, this one is often interconnected with the other Gifts. This is especially true when a prophetic word is spoken. Are they words from God or just nice words? Or is it malevolent in nature?

A classic example of this Gift was exercised by Paul in Philippi (Acts 16). Paul and Silas, while in prayer, encountered a "slave girl possessed with a spirit of divination." She ended up following them for several days crying out, "These men are the servants of the Most High God who proclaim to us the way of salvation."

Having spoken in remote regions of the world, I can tell you that I probably would have welcomed her to my team! It's nice to have a "local" confirm your message. Yet, the presence of a malevolent spirit or spirits can only disrupt what you ultimately want to accomplish.

Whatever the reasons Paul had for waiting to free this young lady from her bondage, he eventually accomplished the task, "I command you in the name of Jesus Christ to come out of her."

How and Why is This Gift Important?

1. This Gift will help you discern the root of what is afflicting a person who is suffering mental disorders. If it truly is demonic influence, knowing that can make all the difference in setting the captive free.

    (See Mark 5:5; Luke 9:39; Acts 5:16)

Like the young woman in Mexico, her trauma most probably opened this door to demonic activity. Dealing with that is the first, albeit critical, step. However, as is often the case, demonic expulsion also requires sensitive follow-up counseling and biblical-based therapy.

2. This Gift will help you discern if there are wolves among the sheep in the body of Christ. Of course, the gift must be applied with great wisdom and maturity.

   (See Acts 13:9-10; 1 John 4:1-6)

   We are instructed to not indiscriminately accept the pronouncements of all prophetic words. What spirit is behind the prophet? We are encouraged to "test."

   > *Beloved, do not believe every spirit, but test the spirits, whether they are of God; because many false prophets have gone out into the world.* 1 John 4:1

3. This Gift will help you discern and expose error. There is such a thing as "lying spirits," seducing spirits that can be responsible for spreading false doctrine:

   > *Now the Spirit expressly says that in the latter times some will depart from the faith, giving heed to deceiving spirits and doctrines of demons.* (1 Timothy 4:1)

   (See also 2 Peter 2)

4. This Gift will help you discern between a godly miracle or healing:

> *The coming of the lawless one is according to the working of Satan, with all power, signs, and lying wonders.* (2 Thessalonians 2:9)

If we truly are in the "last days," this Gift will be needed more and more.

The devil is a counterfeit. I've seen it over and over again. Counterfeits by nature look close to the real thing, but are worse than worthless. They steal from the real thing.

If we truly are in the "last days," this Gift will be needed more and more. Whether it's a charlatan "faith healer" who uses an earpiece to gain "words of knowledge" or the pastor who calls all miracles and healings of the devil, we must remain vigilant. Warning: Some believe they are operating in this Gift when in reality they are motivated by skepticism and suspicion.

5. This Gift will also help you discern if the Spirit of the Lord is residing in someone.

When someone may ask to serve or speak, it's good to ask the Lord regarding their heart and motive. Human behavior is often motivated by the human spirit (which can be damaged) and then influenced by a demonic/satanic spirit or by the Holy Spirit.

When Jesus encountered Nathanael (see John 1:47-48) He, without knowing him, understood his heart, "Behold, an Israelite indeed, in whom is no deceit!" It startled Nathanael who replied, "How do you know me?"

Can You Discern the Spirit by Natural Observation?

This is an important question and the reason I chose to open this section with the account of the young woman in Mexico.

Depending on your background, religious training, and academic level, how you discern what is motivated by the spirits or by a mental disorder will be impacted.

We all have a tendency to perceive reality through our grid of experience and education. The young woman in Mexico, to those experienced in exorcisms, would have taken one look at her and said, "Let's cast this out!" The psychologist or seasoned counselor would say, "Let's interview her to understand her trauma." In fact, both could be correct. Trauma and demonization can go hand-in-hand.

The point is that natural observation can provide a starting point and add to the discerning process. It might have been why

Paul waited to cast out the demon in the young woman in Philippi.

I've had people growl, speak in strange voices, contort, etc. By natural observation, my experience tends toward believing they are demonized. YET, this is where the gift of discernment is so valuable. I never rely on my natural observations and I always ask the Holy Spirit to reveal the true source of the issue.

Shake My Hand!

Sometimes nothing in the natural will indicate an evil spirit, but the believer must always be listening to the Holy Spirit.

I fly to many island nations in the South Pacific – oftentimes into regions where nobody knows me. So, it's common that when I step off a plane, I will be greeted or someone will have a sign with my name on it.

As I stepped off this particular flight, a middle-aged man dressed like all the locals came up to me, someone I've never met before in my life, and reached out to shake my hand.

Because I'm a nice guy, if someone in a foreign country, hopefully there to pick me up, asks to shake my hand, I shake his hand – especially if he insists, "Pastor, shake my hand."

Now I did something I've never done before or since. I said, "No." So rude, isn't it? Yet, something inside me, of course the Holy Spirit, said to decline the offer.

"Don't touch me," I added to my terse "No."

Yet, he insisted again, "Pastor, shake my hand."

He followed me outside the tiny terminal where I would pick up my luggage. I saw someone I knew who greeted me, so I asked him, pointing to the man who wanted to shake my hand, "Who's that man? He knew I was a pastor."

"That guy's a witch doctor," my host replied.

"Well, he really wanted to shake my hand," I said rather sarcastically.

"Because he wanted to put a curse on you," my host responded matter of factly.

I probably knew the answer when I asked the question, but I asked it anyway, "Well, how does he know who I am?"

"He knows who you are. The devil knows who you are."

The unseen battle is real, my friends.

Don't be Deceived

As stated in point 4, the devil is a counterfeiter, a liar. This was never more apparent than during a women's meeting in my home when my wife and I were young pastors.

I had entered into some deep R.E.M. sleep when she woke me about 1:00 in the morning, insisting I help her. After many incoherent protestations, I relented, only to find one of these female leaders from our church manifesting a demon – the whole head turning, scary voice, *Exorcist* thing (by the way, a movie I will never see).

Being young and inexperienced, we didn't have much success. Running out of things to do, we asked the demon it's name.

"Krishna."

I didn't know if it was lying, but suspected it was. After all, the devil is the "father of lies." But we kept praying, because what else were we going to do? Suddenly, she lifted her hands, her eyes looked normal, and she was worshiping.

Everybody started to praise the Lord, "She's delivered!" Then she started to speak in tongues.

"Oh, praise Jesus!"

But I crashed the party, "That's not the Spirit."

Everyone disagreed, "Look, she's worshiping Jesus!" By all natural observations, she spoke and acted like someone perfectly normal. But the gift of discerning of spirits inside me let me know her tongues were counterfeit; in fact, it was demonic.

"I rebuke you in the name of Jesus."

Immediately she went back into contortions and other manifestations. Unfortunately, she wasn't delivered that morning. A sad story, but it reminds me to test the spirit and to trust the Holy Spirit to reveal all truth.

Beware the "Religious" Spirit

One of the roles of any pastor and leader is to protect the flock. Like the actual shepherds that the Bible used as metaphors of spiritual authority, church shepherds must defend from sneak attacks from the enemy. It's serious stuff.

One time, while praying for a group that had gathered in line, many people fell under the weight of the presence of God. However, after one particular woman fell, I grabbed her hand to pull her back up. I didn't know her, yet

> The gift of discerning of spirits is part of the rod and staff each shepherd possesses.

something came out of my mouth and said, "Don't ever do that again."

You can imagine the looks I received. People around her thought I'd lost my mind. She too looked shocked, but I said it again because there were, as the Spirit was revealing to me, many issues that needed to be confronted. They were issues affecting the church, like her prophesying to a much younger man that he was supposed to be her husband instead of her actual spouse.

The gift of discerning of spirits is part of the rod and staff each shepherd possesses. In fact, each believer can move in this Gift to protect the sheep that God fiercely loves.

the GIFT of

FAITH

STEP OUT OF THE BOAT

Mountains

transrational certainty

Assurance that GOD Will Act

MUSTARD SEED

MOVE

YOU KNOW that you KNOW

Chapter Nine

Living the Power Gifts: Gotta Have a Little Faith

Gift of Faith

The news caused me to sit down. I knew my over-reaction would make things worse. Disappointment and anger kept me pinned to the chair. I kept it all inside. I was more mad at myself than at anyone else. Why wasn't I on top of this?

"So we are tens of thousands of dollars short and dozens of students will be forfeiting their airfare unless it's all raised... in 24 hours," I repeated back to my staff the news I just learned, as if they would correct me and tell me it wasn't that bad. We were a short-term mission school, based on the Youth With a Mission model, in a local church. With over 200 students who had graduated from six months of

> The Lord spoke to me, clearly though not audibly, "I am going to give you the gift of faith."

intensive training and discipleship, most were scheduled for various short-term team missions around the world.

There was no time to investigate the whys. The only thing we knew was that we needed a miracle of sorts and to raise a lot of money among mainly poor college and college-aged students. So we prayed.

The Lord spoke to me, clearly though not audibly, "I am going to give you the gift of faith."

I'm embarrassed to say that at the time I wasn't exactly sure what the gift of faith was, but I excitedly told my staff what I believed God had said. Their bemused faces betrayed what we all were thinking. "What is the gift of faith and how is it going to help us raise thousands of dollars tonight?"

As I tend to do in stressful situations, I joked, "I wish He had said He was going to give us the Gift of Money."

Yet, as the students began to fill the room for the evening meeting, the staff came in, not in panic, but with a strange peace.

Money, Money, Money

The evening started as most others – a wonderful time of worship. As I walked up to the podium, I still had no idea what the Lord wanted to do. All I knew was His promise to give us the gift of faith. By then, I had at least found the 1 Corinthians

12 scripture, but still lacked anything but a simple understanding.

I shared our dilemma with the entire school: being thousands of dollars short, less than 24 hours to go, and many students still lacking funds. But I told them the word of the Lord, "God has promised to give us the gift of faith."

I asked any student that lacked funds to raise their hand. As dozens of hands lifted throughout the room, I invited the Holy Spirit to come and thanked Him for the gift He had promised to release. I realized later this might have been a word of wisdom. And often the Gifts synchronize together.

Without any prompting, students began going up to those whose hands were raised and giving them money. They'd slip checks or cash into their pockets. It seemed entirely spontaneous – no words, just occasional hugs, and it went on for minutes.

Then it became even more extraordinary. Students with raised hands began giving their newly acquired funds to others – both with hands raised and not. Some students gave away everything they had just received to someone else, and then someone would bless them back. It went back and forth for nearly an hour. The room filled with a joy, a sheer hilarity of giving, laughter, tears, astonishment, but more than anything – faith.

In the end, not only did every single student/missionary have enough money for their trip, but we also had $7,000 extra to bless the nations we visited. Not bad for a room full of mainly poor college students.

So What is the Gift of Faith?

That night I experienced the power of faith, but also an important lesson. Every believer walks in certain levels of faith. Some, much like the disciple Thomas, run low at times; others are willing to jump out of the boat and into the lake when they see Jesus. And none of that faith is static. You can be Bold Peter in one minute and Sinking Peter in another.

But sometimes God intervenes. He desires for His purpose (and His pleasure, I believe) to gift His people with an entirely different level of faith. It is the kind of faith required to see the blind see, the deaf hear, the dead resurrect, but also the homeless to receive a home, the drug addict to be set free, the prostitute to leave their old life.

"This gift (faith) is a supernatural surge of confidence from the Spirit of God which arises within a person faced with a specific situation or need whereby that person receives a trans-rational certainty and assurance that God is about to act through a word or action."[1] (David Pytches)

I just love the phrase "trans-rational certainty."

Jesus, in Matthew 17:20, gives what could be considered a word of wisdom to his disciples regarding faith. They had just viewed one of the most remarkable miracles in the Bible, the Transfiguration. Instead of being full of faith to cast out the demon in the epileptic boy, they failed.

Embarrassed, they sought Jesus out for a private conversation, "Why could we not cast it out?" His answer, direct and instructive, "Because of your unbelief." Then Jesus gave His disciples a key to the Kingdom that is as true today as it was when He spoke:

> *I say to you, if you have faith as a mustard seed, you will say to this mountain, "Move from here to there," and it will move; and nothing will be impossible for you.*

Obviously, the mountain was a metaphor for a huge obstacle; but Jesus instills in the disciples the need for, and desire for, an increasing personal faith. This is a topic for much more discussion. The spectrum of teaching on faith swings wide.

What is clear from Jesus' answer: we all possess faith. We should exercise whatever degree of it we have and we must believe that our faith (in Him) can grow — even to see God do extraordinary things. However, the gift of faith is the supernatural intervention of belief that supersedes even our own faith and enables us to move in the faith desired by God.

There's a wonderful and instructive sidebar to this story. After both challenging the disciples' personal faith and then raising it with a powerful promise, He states, almost off the cuff:

> *However, this kind does not go out except by prayer and fasting.* Matthew 17:21

It's almost as if Jesus is saying, yes, with more faith the demon should have been cast out, but don't be totally discouraged – some demons (and situations) require prayer and fasting. Why? Prayer and fasting are spiritual disciplines that draw you closer to the Lord. Prayer and fasting will build your faith. You may not always possess such faith, but there is a way the Father has shown us to increase our faith – pray and fast.

And when you pray and fast (and this is my interpretation) the Spirit of God will give (grace) you a special ability, a gift, specifically that of faith which will be in agreement with God to unlock authority and power in the spiritual realm.

Faith is that thing that brings us into alignment with the Kingdom.

You will be seeing that which the Father is doing. You won't be acting as a free agent, a lone ranger, but as an ambassador of the Kingdom of God, speaking words that are in full agreement with Kingdom principles and the very heart of God – to see on earth as it is in heaven.

Faith is that thing that brings us into alignment with the Kingdom. And anything that ever comes from it, being a blind eye opening or a "mountain" moving, is never just our faith, but our cooperation with that which the Father is doing.

George Muller said it so well:

"Faith does not operate in the realm of the possible. Faith begins where man's power ends."[2]

Faith and Grace

God's rewards are of grace, not merit – it is a key Kingdom principle that our flesh fights and our mind struggles to accept. Author Francois Du Toit says it well:

"Faith is not something we do to persuade God, faith is what happens to us when we realize how persuaded God is about us."[3]

Position yourself to grow in faith by growing in grace, knowing that every good work comes from the Father and that apart from Him we can do absolutely nothing.

Do we grow in grace by striving – by impressing God with all of our efforts? Of course not. We grow by spending time with the Master, by being at His feet with ear and heart inclined to His voice.

The same is true of faith. Faith is, in a sense, the extension of grace. It is the gift from God to see His Kingdom established. Walk in God's grace and faith will flow. However, please do not confuse receiving grace with some kind of spiritual state, requiring no further action. Our walk is full of choices. I love the quote from A.W. Tozer:

"If we are not changed by grace, then we are not saved by grace."[4]

Moving in the Gift of Faith

There is obvious overlap in growing (and learning) in faith and moving (receiving) in the gift of faith. And at times, the two will be indistinguishable.

The spectrum of faith is wide. Even before trusting in Christ, we may have had a

All the other disciples in the boat had some faith, but it was Peter who had a surge of faith that allowed him to actually step from a dry boat into wet water.

certain amount of faith to believe in God. We grow in our relationship with the Father and begin to trust Him in everyday aspects of life. Of course, trust and faith are interconnected. It's hard to trust something or someone you don't have faith in, or vice versa for that matter.

But there are times you may be aware of where you had, for lack of a better phrase, "a surge of" faith. We've all experienced the opposite – a surge of doubt. The often-used example of Peter in the boat – he almost simultaneously experienced both. He had faith. All the other disciples in the boat had some faith, but it was Peter who had a surge of faith that allowed him to actually step from a dry boat into wet water.

There is No Explanation for This

When Shavonne Lang, a long time member of Pastors Huey and Ruth Hudson's Restoration Church in Alabama, completed surgery for breast cancer she decided to celebrate. A long ordeal in a life full of physical challenges had ended. She was grateful to the doctors and staff, and thankful for the Lord's guiding hand.

Soon after the celebration, pain found its way back into the right side of Shavonne's body, so excruciating it forced her to the emergency room. The news crushed her: a tumor in her kidney.

"I did not want to believe that report." So she sought out four different urologists, but all came to the same conclusion: more surgery.

Devastated, but still clinging to hope, Shavonne listened one Sunday morning in church to a powerful message on miracles. Pastor Ruth Hudson saw her and called her down for prayer.

"We're going to pray for your miracle," Pastor Ruth spoke firmly, as someone who knew firsthand the power of God. Along with another member of the church, they prayed powerfully, declaring to Shavonne, "You're healed! Just believe it!"

Reminded of the parable of the mustard seed in Matthew 17, she received and believed, "Lord, please move this mountain."

There are those in the Body of Christ who would discourage such pronouncements of healing prior to conclusive evidence. There are rightful concerns about presumption. No one wants to further damage the already weakened emotional state of people in pain.

And then, there are times when faith rises even in the face of all the scientific evidence. Shavonne had a tumor on her right kidney. The x-rays didn't lie. How dare someone proclaim otherwise – unless, of course, God said.

"Now faith is the substance of things hoped for, the evidence of things not seen." (Hebrews 11:1)

Shavonne walked into the doctor's office full of emotions, but also holding on dearly to faith. "Did you have surgery at Vanderbilt?" The physician referenced the medical center at the well-known university. Shavonne thought he might be referring to her breast surgery. "Did I do the surgery?" he further inquired.

Perplexed, the doctor proclaimed, "Well, somebody did the surgery!" Showing her the side-by-side x-rays, one with the kidney tumor and one with a "divot" where the tumor used to be, he conceded, "There's no explanation for this."

God's hand, more skillful than any surgeon's, still operates today. When He moves, how He moves, even why He moves in such dramatic ways causes even the skeptics to inquire about faith in God. We as believers know that even faith in its smallest form affects the very emotions of God, for the Scripture is clear:

"Without faith it is impossible to please God."
(Hebrews 11:6)

God was pleased to heal Shavonne.

The Miracle Child

"The Lord says you are completely healed. You will surely have the child in your arms by this time next year." It only took a few minutes for my lips that just uttered such a faith-filled prayer to mutter under my breath, "What a stupid thing to say. I can't believe I said that."

Just the night before, I had successfully fought off one of the most visually disturbing demonic apparitions I've ever encountered before or since. So, as I entered this barren Fijian woman's home, I had great faith. But without question, it took the gift of faith from the Holy Spirit to surge through me in the moment I laid hands on her and opened my mouth.

God had great plans for her, her husband, and the surrounding village. I just needed to be obedient and speak, in faith, the words He had given me.

One year later, my wife and I were in the same area preaching. Just before I was about to share my message, a woman came running up to me holding a baby and shouting, "Pastor! Pastor, look!" Though I did not initially recognize her, she told me that only one week after the prayer she became pregnant. She gave all the glory to God.

But, that's only half of the story. Upon returning to this village a decade later, I learned that her testimony really impacted the people, 90% of whom were non-believers. Because of her healing, nearly everyone in the village came to Christ.

She wasn't simply barren; she lacked any reproductive organs, according to her visits to numerous doctors. No one doubted the creative hand of God, and they responded accordingly. I doubted after my prayer, but faith had already been released. I simply spoke of that which the Father was doing.

> God is looking for his Church to say what he is speaking and to do what he is doing – nothing more, nothing less.

God is looking for His Church to say what He is speaking and to do what He is doing – nothing more, nothing less.

5 Steps to Greater Faith

Though we should expect the gift of faith to move through us at times, we need to build our faith to move mountains. We should always be growing in our faith walk. And, I've found that the gift of faith often moves in us after we take that first step of faith. Here are five keys I've always followed:

1. **Walk in the faith you have.**

   We all start somewhere. Even the saving faith to believe in Christ was a gift from God.

   > *For by grace you have been saved by faith, and that not of yourself; it is the gift of God...*" **Ephesians 2:8**

   You'll soon realize, if you haven't already, that if you are truly walking in faith, you are growing in faith. What you struggled to have faith for six months ago may seem easier today. The key is that any faith you do have is a gift – there is no room for pride.

2. **Build your faith from learning the Word.**

   Romans 10:17 couldn't be any clearer:

   > *So then faith comes by hearing and hearing by the Word of God.*

   No shortcut – wish there was, but there isn't. You build your faith by reading and then internalizing the Word of God. You also build your faith by trusting in the promises of Scripture. Act on the Word, see God move – faith grows.

   Do you "feel" abandoned by God? What did Jesus tell us? "I will never leave you or forsake you." Knowing the Scripture, not only key verses, but full context to understand the nature of God, His Son, your sin, etc. gives you both a path and a purpose to your journey.

Thy word is a lamp unto my feet and a light unto my path. **Psalm 119:105**

3. **Let people of faith impart faith into your life.**

In 2 Timothy 1:5, Paul makes an interesting observation about Timothy:

I call to remembrance the genuine faith that is in you which dwelt first in your grandmother Lois and your mother Eunice and I am persuaded is in you also.

Sometimes the greatest, yet most ignored, people of faith are our family. Cherish that praying grandmother or caring father. Allow them to speak into your life.

Dr. Leslie Keegel, someone with a legitimate apostolic ministry, credits this to the times he would watch and learn from his Holy Spirit-sensitive grandmother.

> "My grandmother, although uneducated, moved in the anointing of God as powerfully as anyone I've ever met... I would often sit by her closed door to listen to her prayers. Every morning before school, I went to her to get prayer and an anointing of oil."[5]

If family is not able, and even if they are, seek out people who move in a level of faith that you desire. Of course, be cautious and discerning. If they seem to move in the Gifts but lack in the fruit of the Spirit, steer clear.

In a day and age where we are terrified of ever judging anyone else, the Psalmist says in chapter one, verse one:

> *Blessed is the man who walks not in the counsel of the ungodly, nor stands in the path of sinners, nor sits in the seat of the scornful.*

Who and what are filling our hearts, our minds? I know it can sound overly simplistic, but we make a choice, often daily, to decide to whom we will listen. Will it be people walking in fear or people walking in faith? If you think you're stronger than your environment, and being surrounded by doubt and skepticism won't impact your faith – please reconsider. Or if you live in circumstances that prevent you from leaving, then ask God, daily, hourly, to guard your heart and mind – putting on the full armor of God.

Seek those who will impart faith into you. God gave Joshua the faith to see the sun stop, but it didn't hurt for Joshua to have walked with Moses for 40 years.

4. **Build your faith by praying in the Spirit.**

A week after receiving my prayer language (that's a book in itself) I found myself involved in an exorcism – yes, a person manifesting, contorting, and basically freaking me out. Things of the Spirit were new to me, but walking into the house where the exorcism was to take place, I found myself immediately on my knees praying in tongues. The presence of evil was very real. At that moment, the Lord spoke to my heart that a whole new spiritual realm would now be open to me and that I had opened the door to it by speaking in tongues. In fact, I moved in multiple gifts of the Spirit that day, and my life was never the same.

Jude 1:20 says:

> *But you, beloved, building yourselves up on your most holy faith, praying in the Holy Spirit...*

Praying in the Spirit, moving in the discerning of spirits, and the word of knowledge served me well as we ministered to this demonized person. I was neither aware of these Gifts, other than tongues, nor had I asked for them; but God in His mercy for this person (and probably for me too!) graced me with them. These were the first small steps in a large walk of faith.

We all need first steps. David said yes to the opportunity to kill Goliath. Did that happen in a vacuum? Of course not, he had faith in God because he saw God's faithfulness when he slayed the lion and the bear.

5. **Never give up.**

Walking by faith, not by sight, is not easy. It wasn't intended to be. Sometimes all your empirical senses will scream "No!" yet the Spirit speaking to your spirit will say "Yes." Learning how to listen to that inner voice will be critical in your journey as a believer. How to distinguish the voice of the Lord from other "voices" will be essential.

The Bible says in 1 Corinthians 16:13,

> *Watch, stand fast in the faith, be brave, be strong.*

In Ephesians 6, Paul encourages every believer to be strong in the Lord and to put on the whole armor of God – and to stand firm.

In verse 16 he says:

> *Above all, taking the shield of faith...*

And ending with verse 18 he states:

> *praying always with all prayer and supplication in the Spirit...*

The Hebrew hall of faith is filled with those who never gave up. The Lord Himself set the ultimate example of perseverance – even to the cross.

Grow continually in your faith in God. Be always open to the Holy Spirit's gift of faith. Both are pleasing to the Lord.

BUILD a **LIFE** Style

The GIFTS of **HEALING**

PRAY FOR IT!

LISTEN to the SPIRIT

DON'T QUIT

BELIEVE

GOD's HEART is to Heal

Chapter Ten

Living the Power Gifts: Be Healed!

The Gifts of Healings[1]

As our small boat raced over the chopping waters of an Amazon River tributary, my mind too raced with both fear and faith. Our destination: an isolated island where an older, blind woman lived with her deaf husband. Our purpose: to pray for her healing.

The team I was leading had seen quite a few healings since we had arrived in Brazil some three weeks before. In fact, not one of the dozens that we prayed for seemed to have left untouched by the Spirit. We were diligent to interview everyone, asking them to describe both their afflictions and how they believed God had healed them.

Some healings we simply took the word of the person healed. Other healings were visually evident – like large goiters that shrank or people bent over now standing straight. Deaf ears opened and we tested the hearing, praying until the hearing seemed normal. Faces in pain, ranging from toothache to headache, were now full of joy.

A prophetic word from someone in our church, deeply respected for her accuracy, promised this would occur. Honestly, though I appreciated the word, I gave it little importance, until the Lord reminded me of it after His outpouring among these people living on the banks of the Amazon.

And none of us on this short-term mission team had ever seen such healing. We were continually in awe, asking the people who were healed, "Are you sure?" We asked not as a statement of doubt, but wanting not to leave them until they were completely healed. In fact, a local elder said to me after a service when dozens were healed, "Why would God send you all this way if He wasn't coming with you?" As we docked our boat on the muddy shoreline, I hoped and prayed He would be with me one more time.

She looked older than I had anticipated, although river people's weathered skin often defied their true age. Immediately, as we were being introduced by our guide through my interpreter, I saw the infected eye. I had heard she was blind, but not due to such a severe infection. Seeing it did nothing to build my faith. In fact, I later joked that I watched my faith float down the Amazon after looking at that eye. But, we had come a long way; the least we could do was pray for her.

Jesus never did random healings or miracles. Everything had a purpose. That's why the blind man in Mark 8:22-25 is so intriguing, instructive, and unique:

> Then He came to Bethsaida; and they brought a blind man to Him, and begged Him to touch him. So He took the blind man by the hand and led him out of the town. And when He had spit on his eyes and put His hands on him, He asked him if he saw anything. And he looked up and said, "I see men like trees, walking." Then He put His hands on his eyes again and made him look up. And he was restored and saw everyone clearly.

This encounter with the blind man followed closely with his healing of the deaf mute man in which he spoke "Ephphatha," that is, "Be opened" – but only after he put his fingers in his ears, followed up by spitting (on his fingers) and putting them on this man's tongue.

A lot of spitting. The Roman writer, Pliny the Elder, writing in the 1st Century, mentions the curative content of spittle. However, at the time of Christ, Jews generally viewed spit as offensive (see also Deuteronomy 25:9) as we do today.

Theologians have suggested Jesus' intentions were metaphorical in nature, a picture of the disciples' lack of complete understanding of Jesus. I believe it was simply modeling the life of resurrection power that Jesus promised for us.

Here are five practical insights to this scripture and how Jesus modeled to us how to pray for the sick.

1. When praying for the sick, be prepared to take time. Not all healing is instantaneous. Look for the little things. Don't be discouraged if nothing happens immediately. If nothing happens, don't manufacture it. It's not about you or your reputation.

2. Your surroundings can impact the healing process. (E.g., in a room full of fear, lack of faith, or even loved ones being over-protective)

   So He took the blind man... and led him out of the town. **Mark 8:23a**

   (It can also be argued from this scripture that Jesus took him away because he did not want others to see this miracle.)

3. He "interviewed" him during the healing process.

   He asked him if he saw anything. **Mark 8:23b**

Don't be afraid to keep your eyes open, both physically and spiritually, and watch what the Holy Spirit is doing.

4. Listen to the Holy Spirit. How is He telling you to pray? In this case, Jesus knew He was to use an unusual physical point of contact – His hands and spit. Jesus, obviously, didn't routinely use spittle. The lesson here is to not be locked into a method, but into listening to the Spirit.

5. Keep praying until the Holy Spirit releases you. Even Jesus prayed a second time (the only time He did so) – not because of His lack of healing power. It could have been a need to bolster the faith of the blind man, or more probably, model another healing scenario for the disciples (and eventually you and me). Yet, don't fall prey to a model of prayer that says to pray louder and longer if nothing happens. Be quiet so you can listen to the Spirit.

> Unfortunately, we often want Jesus to heal on our terms.

(See Mark 6:5 as an example where the lack of faith impacted the healing process.)

Unfortunately, we often want Jesus to heal on our terms. We want big, powerful, complete or not at all. Yet, the Kingdom principle is that the Lord gives more to those who are faithful in the small things. Sometimes the healing process does not fit our paradigm on healing. It may start with a small change. Remain faithful and keep praying.

Back to the Amazon

Without touching the infected eye, we began to lay hands on this poor woman, my hand moving a mere inch or so above her eye. I prayed in English, my translator in Portuguese.

Something began to occur in our spirits and souls. Faith began to grow. Though we didn't see any evidence of healing on our first prayer, we sensed this would take some time.

In the "second round" of prayer, after removing my hand, I looked closely at the infected eye, searching for any signs of improvement. With it being initially red and swollen, with pus both fresh and crusted – any change would be welcomed. The translator looked at me with a smile, "I think it's getting better." Both our faith and determination grew.

This back and forth of prayer and observation went on for probably 45 minutes. Each time we saw improvement. Eventually, the skin around the eye was completely pink and healthy. So we asked her if her sight was restored – it was. We tested her by having her cover the other eye and having her call out the number of fingers we raised at various distances.

We stood there stunned, in awe of participating in an act of Almighty God. But then, something happened that might have tested even the faith of the apostle Paul. She rather matter-of-factly proclaimed it was her other eye that was completely blind. The first eye was blind due to the infection. Our faith-filled delirium drained from our hearts and washed out on the white sandy beach.

I quickly got over my irritated "Why didn't she tell us?" because I knew we hadn't asked; we assumed. Not wise when praying for healing.

So, we prayed for the other eye. Not so full of faith, but full of something equally as powerful: "God, we are drained, empty. We can only completely depend upon you." It's an interesting spiritual and emotional phenomenon when you "feel" full of faith compared to feeling "I got nothing." I realize critics of healing may pounce on the declaration of "feelings," but as humans, we cannot avoid the emotional side of healing. Sometimes we sense a partnership and participate, other times we are like an unwitting conduit or casual observer.

This time it "felt" as if we would lay on our hands, but it would not be so much us being the vehicle of His power as us watching from front row seats. We knew, however, that God had this; so we prayed, seeing once again sight being slowly restored after every prayer. Soon the other eye saw clearly. She received total healing from blindness.

It's almost a footnote to this wonderful story that after her healing she reminded us of her deaf husband. Almost as if to say, "Why not, God's on a roll," we prayed for him and thankfully his healing took much less time. We got back in our boat after hugs and words of thankfulness. Interestingly, and worth noting for purposes of this book, the enemy immediately tried to place doubt in my heart as we motored away, waving to the couple. "Did what happened actually happen?"

Thankfully, my interpreter and our guide would not let us forget. God still heals today.

Keep Your Eyes Open!

After years of praying for the sick, I most often keep my eyes open to see if there is anything I can observe during the healing process. Sometimes you can see a certain radiance in the face, or eyelids that flutter, maybe stiffness or shaking. It doesn't necessarily mean healing is taking place, but is often an indicator.

In one particular situation, I literally chased pain throughout the body of a fellow minister. It actually became humorous, especially when it left his body. Without the observation and interview process, I wouldn't have been directed to pray specifically over the spot of pain.

Here's a story from a highly respected missionary, Joyce Butron, describing the need for observation.

> "When I was a young college student, I went on my first short-term missions trip, sent out by my university to spend three months in Trinidad, Tobago and St. Lucia. Just prior to going on the trip, my father gave me a very important piece of advice. He told me, 'Joyce, when you pray for someone to be healed, keep your eyes open so you can see what God is doing.'

> "A few days after he gave me that advice, we were in a small church perched at the top of a very steep hill. It was raining very hard and we were in a building with a corrugated metal roof. We could hardly hear each other because the rain was falling so strongly on the roof. The road was knee deep in mud. There was a bucket of water at the front door so you could wash the mud off of your legs before coming into the church.

> "As the service was beginning, a woman arrived carrying a small boy on her back. The service proceeded and then an altar call was given for people who wanted to ask Jesus into their lives and for others who needed

prayer for healing. This woman came forward for prayer. She explained that she was a single mom who had several children to care for. She also told us she worked as a laundress.

"Earlier that day, while washing clothes in the river, she had slipped and fallen, landing on some rocks. This fall had resulted in a broken arm. She told us she had walked about five miles with her 5-year-old son on her back through the rain and mud because she needed Jesus to heal her. She had no money for a doctor and her children would have no food if she was not able to work. She knew she could not wash clothes with only one arm.

> We could see the broken pieces of the bones pushing up against the swollen skin of her arm.

"We listened to her and said, 'Let's pray.' I remembered what my father said as we held her broken arm in the palm of our hands. We could see the broken pieces of the bones pushing up against the swollen skin of her arm. She winced as we held her arm as gently as we could, and we began to pray. As we prayed, I kept my eyes wide open and I saw the bones move back into place, the swelling dissipate, and as we said 'Amen,' she moved her arm, declared it was healed and pain-free, picked up her son, and walked home.

"The Holy Spirit was at work healing and I was privileged to cooperate with what He was doing and watch His power at work."

Like the rest of the Gifts, you can put yourself in a position to move in the gift of healing.

1. **Put yourself in the position to see God heal by praying for healing.** Stating the obvious? Yes, but the truth is few believers consistently put themselves in a situation where they lay hands on the sick. They may lob an "I'm praying for you" over Facebook, but will they actually meet with the individual and ask God to heal? This is such a critical first step. You have to put yourself out there – fear of failure and all. And, by the way, be open to praying outside the church or home. Cannot God be present on the deli aisle of your supermarket?

I've seen more failure in praying for the sick than success, but there's a big reason I've seen so many more healings and miracles than the average pastor. It's point number two…

2. **Don't quit.** I simply won't stop praying for healing, for deliverances, for God to show up. I'm a pit bull for Jesus!

Why? Because I've learned to get over myself, my pride, my fears, my prestige, and focus entirely upon "that which the Father is doing." And actually, once you cross that proverbial "Rubicon," it's liberating. It's no longer about me, but Him. I don't get the glory when He heals and I don't take the blame when He doesn't.

I say this all the time: If you don't pray, things won't happen.

I say this all the time: If you don't pray, things won't happen.

3. **Get it in your heart – it is God's nature to heal.** Never do you read in the Bible Jesus saying it's not His desire to heal. Only the "unbelief" cited in the Mark 6:5 passage indicates the blockage of "mighty works," but even a "few sick people" were healed. God's heart is to heal. Why we don't see more healing is not God's problem – it's ours. Yet, even Jesus, when healing the man at the Pool of Bethesda, could have healed the others waiting at this same pool. But He didn't. The Father was only directing Him to this specific man.

    The key to praying for the sick is hearing from the Father. But sometimes you don't hear His voice and still we must pray. The flow of healing can be a mystery, but not the instructions from the Lord to pray for healing. We live in a fallen world, but serve the King of Kings.

I remember early in my marriage when my wife became violently ill. She refused to go to the hospital and I prayed like never before. I prayed as hard as I ever have – yet nothing. She got even sicker. Though she recovered within 24 hours, the experience set me back to the point I stopped praying. Maybe that's where you are now.

It took time, but I began to realize I would never see another sick or hurt person ever recover again if I didn't start to pray. Little by little, faith returned – small but critical steps of faith. I suppose if every time we prayed for healing that it occurred, faith would no longer be a needed ingredient. But, along with our faith, we must never lose sight of the sovereignty of God. He is in charge. He knows why and when and if. And if that healing takes place during the passage from earth to eternity – it will take place. He wants all to be healed and how is not up to us; but the fact is He uses us to pray and believe for it. To do anything less is outside His will.

In retrospect, I believe my pride was hurt when God did not instantly heal my wife. "Man of God" couldn't heal his own bride. That's right – I couldn't and never will be able to.

Only He can; and sometimes He doesn't heal exactly as we want Him to.

What If in Prayer He Says "No" to Healing

It is rare, but I have prayed for people when the Lord let me know that they would not be healed. I've never felt comfortable sharing that with their loved ones, of course, partially due to a desire to be proactive and comforting and partially due to the fact that I could have heard from God incorrectly. There can always be a greater objective that God intends that we cannot discern.

One of my closest friends, and key leader in my church, was the standard of health. He regularly exercised and thought nothing of going on up to a 100-mile bike ride. Yet, one day after we both had attended a funeral he blurted out, "The Lord just told me I'm next."

I immediately rebuked him, "Absolutely not! You're not going to die." Yet everyday he came to me saying the same thing asking me to pray for him and prepare him for the next life.

A month later, stricken with an illness called Guillain-Barre', he entered into a comatose state. I still didn't believe this was of God, and with full faith commanded the illness to leave his body. I never believed so hard for anyone. Only after the Lord spoke to my stubborn heart did I relent, "No, he's at home with Me and he doesn't want to come back."

God's will must always be interpreted in light of eternity. If healing does not take place for the believer on this earth, it will immediately upon the next life. This is not a "cop out," but an enlightened view of life as eternal.

Because we do not fully see this eternal equation, we are instructed to pray in faith in this life for healing. We are never instructed to be passive in the face of sickness or the demonic. In fact, we are to model Jesus. He saw hundreds healed and delivered by always seeking to do that which the Father is doing. There are times the Father's healing hand is on someone and times when it is not. As disciples, we hope to be in step with Him, hearing His voice and praying accordingly.

But, because we see through "a glass dimly" we should always pray for healing and total deliverance – never "hedging our bets" with an "if it be thy will" type of prayer that on its face seems pious, but was never modeled by Jesus, certainly not to His disciples. According to Bill Johnson:

"In the thousands of people I've seen healed, I've never seen anyone healed from that kind of prayer."[2]

What if Someone I Pray for is Not Healed?

If you pray for the sick, you will face disappointments as I mentioned before. John Wimber, reminiscing on his first few hundred prayer-for-the-sick attempts, recalls not only seeing no one healed, but sometimes personally experiencing their illness. I've personally prayed for thousands to be healed, yet have only seen hundreds do so.

> Healing is often a process. Your prayer may begin the healing process and you may or may not get to see the completion.

It takes a fighter's mentality. If you can't get up after a blow, you shouldn't be in the ring. Here are some things to keep in mind:

1. Healing is often a process. Your prayer may begin the healing process and you may or may not get to see the completion. Don't get discouraged – sometimes the process will occur in one sitting, other times over a few sittings.

2. Be willing to grow. Learn from others who have moved in the gifts of healing. You may be doing some things that are adversely impacting your ministry.

3. Be willing to fast and pray for healing as a LIFESTYLE. Learn from those times in the Spirit.

4. If someone is not healed, do not take it personally. There are many factors involved in the healing process. Not all of it involves the person praying.

5. Never blame the person you are praying for. There may be things discerned through the other Gifts that are impacting the healing process, but let love and compassion lead you.

6. Possibly, we don't experience healing because the Lord wants us to see a doctor. Operating in the gifts of healing does not mean it's divine healing or nothing. God uses physicians, nurses, and healing practitioners to be His hands.

Good friend, Dr. Steve Schell, believes deeply in the gifts of healing and also believes in listening to the Holy Spirit if He says, "Go to the doctor." A series of divinely orchestrated events recently led Steve to the operating table, involving triple bypass surgery. He was profoundly grateful not only for God's intervention in identifying the critical condition and successful surgery but for all the compassionate care given. According to Steve, God's hand guided the entire process of healing as much as if He had decided to heal instantaneously.

The key? Always be listening to the voice of the Holy Spirit.

Practical Insights Into the Ministry of Healing and Application of the Gift of Healing

1. Rest in the fact that it is God's nature to heal.

2. Trust in His ability and His gifting. All authority is in Jesus, who commissions us to pray for healing.

3. Listen to what the Holy Spirit is doing and saying.

4. Recognize when the Spirit is on a person and be observant both empirically and in the Spirit.

5. Be open to words of knowledge, words of wisdom, and discerning of spirits when praying.

6. Always be compassionate, respecting the individual and keeping everything confidential.

7. Be willing to take as much time as needed in the process.

8. Realize healing is not often instantaneous; be willing to observe, and talk to the individual during the process.

9. Make sure the setting is appropriate for prayer.

10. Be prepared to anticipate distractions before, during, and after prayer.

11. Always give God the glory and be thankful for the privilege to be used by Him.

A Final Word on the Gifts of Healing

Because we live in the kingdom of the "already, but not yet," we all will experience disease, suffering, and eventually death. Yet, being warriors in the Kingdom we fight against these things. We battle in prayer, in faith, believing God's Word. We ask in faith for healing of disease, an end to suffering, and even "No" to death. But when God is silent to any of life's real challenges, we never lose trust in Him. In fact, even in the silence we can hear His voice.

> But when God is silent to any of life's real challenges, we never lose trust in Him. In fact, even in the silence we can hear His voice.

Please read these two stories and allow the Spirit to take you to a deeper understanding of His mercy.

Mike

Mike served as a platoon sergeant in Vietnam. Though never wounded during battle he, like so many returning GIs, suffered the insults and indifference from a war weary nation. He quickly assimilated back into society, earned his degree, married, and had children. Bright and a hard worker, providing for his family never posed a problem, as exemplified by the beautiful home he and my sister bought in Yuba City, California.

An expert in plant diseases, he assisted the many walnut and other tree growers in the rural area of Northern California. They warmed up to this smart but blunt family man. After all, farmers preferred the no-nonsense approach to business and living.

Mike and his entire family gave their hearts to Christ and served the church faithfully. The depth of their faith brought many to their doorstep for prayer, counsel, and an enlightened cup of coffee.

Then, one day, while driving his truck to one of his customer's groves he had an accident, no fault of his own, but his life would never be the same. Back surgery would only make his pain worse – the

Crippling pain may have taken his ability to work, but not to seek God.

doctor operated on the wrong vertebra. Unable to work and barely able to walk, pain became his constant companion – it would never leave. Over the years, Mike's disability drove him not to despair or depression, though he battled each at times, but to a deeper, richer walk with God.

There are few people who I can talk with for literally hours about Jesus. Part of that is probably my own immaturity, but some is the superficiality or religiousness that stunts the conversation. Never with Mike. How often do you have the privilege to speak with another human being who spends hours at the throne of God? Crippling pain may have taken his ability to work, but not to seek God.

When I speak with my brother-in-law, I'm reminded of the scripture in Acts 4:13,

> *When they saw the boldness of Peter and John, and perceived that they were uneducated and untrained men, they marveled. And they realized that they had been with Jesus.*

No Bible college or seminary, only intimate and copious time with Jesus.

Mike has seen God heal. He has moved mightily in the gifts of the Spirit. Yet Mike, to this day, is not healed. He suffers in pain daily, hourly. We who consider ourselves practitioners of this gift struggle with the obvious question: "Why aren't all healed?"

Though some may hide behind dogmatic declarations or selective scriptures, we are faced with the reality – all are not healed and good people suffer.

There is a place in the Kingdom for suffering. Jesus himself has been called the "Suffering Servant." We must, however, be aware of the difference between suffering and sickness. This is not semantics. There seems to be "no indication in the New Testament that suffering means or involves sickness."[3] Yet, it is true that even though sickness draws people closer to God, it is not in the sickness where the virtue lies, but in God's desire for intimacy.

Suffering, however, is presented by the writers of both the Old and New Testaments as part of the believer's experience. It is indisputable that people, like Mike, have drawn closer to God through their suffering. Corrie Ten Boom rightly states:

"The deepest fellowship with Him lies in not resisting when suffering comes our way but in going through it resolutely with Him."[4]

Paul, in one of his most eloquent and contrasting passages, wrote:

That I may know Him and the power of His resurrection, and the fellowship of His sufferings... Philippians 3:10

Paul, of course, isn't asking God for sickness; in fact, he routinely prayed for its elimination. But he is stating the inevitable occurrence: suffering in the lives of New Testament believers.

Anglican Bishop Todd Hunter, well acquainted with the struggles of healing in his own life and with that of his wife, writes insightfully:

"There's a mystery at the intersection of suffering and healing. It's a mystery that's not solved by thinking bad things about God…"

Dr. Hunter, who has also experienced "incredible healings," goes on:

"In fact, the mystery is not actually solved – it's lived into… We live into this mystery by holding God as awesome in our minds, coming to him always, and if not receiving what we want in the way or time we want it, counting on him to someday make sense of our suffering."[5]

> If we are to embrace the Gifts, move in the Spirit, and walk in the power and presence of God, we must remain keenly aware of the human condition.

If we are to embrace the Gifts, move in the Spirit, and walk in the power and presence of God, we must remain keenly aware of the human condition: human frailty, struggles and sufferings – yes, even sin. To gloss over it cheapens the depth of God's grace and mutes the power of the cross.

It also denies the need for the Incarnation – the miracle of the God of the universe desiring to so identify with His creation that He decides to walk with us as fallen humans. To be His disciple, Jesus asks us to do the same in our own limited way. Identify with His power, but in doing so, not to run away from, but embrace, His suffering.

Mike understood this. Though even with a daily routine of hours in the presence of the most Holy God, he would say, "I still see through a glass dimly."

Floyd and Sally

Sickness since The Fall is part of the human experience. No one escapes its clutches. So we pray, as we are instructed in the Word, for healing. We are told to pray in faith even if doubt wants to whisper in our ear. We rely on the Word, listen to the Spirit, and ask in the name of Jesus. We trust the outcome to Him, for in fact, we are all imperfect, even greatly flawed conduits of His power. But we don't pray weakly, hedging our bets, because that was never modeled by Jesus or His disciples.

We step out of the proverbial boat fixing our eyes on Jesus even when the storm of sickness surrounds us. Like the Allied soldier going into battle after D-Day, the victory over the Nazis was assumed, but the bloody battles, until Hitler's fall, remained.

Praying for the sick can get "bloody." Ministry gets messy, bruising at times. Failure happens, battles are lost, but the soldier fights on.

One of my heroes from afar is Floyd McClung. As a former Youth With a Mission student I sat under his anointed teachings and saw first-hand his amazing work in Amsterdam.

A couple of years ago, Floyd went into septic shock, an infection that he still battles to this day. If anyone has received prayers for healing, strong prayers, not weak ones, it's Floyd. He is revered throughout the world as a leader among leaders.

Yet, Floyd remains unhealed as of this writing. His faithful wife, Sally, has written about the experience together. She herself is a cancer survivor so she knows the real struggle from every perspective. Her words are so very insightful as to suffering. They would be words my brother-in-law, Mike, would agree with.

> "There has been a depth of fellowship with the Lord the last few years that is beyond anything I have known. Of course, I've needed Him so much more too! The pain, the need has pressed me in close to His heart in such a precious way.

> "I've found so much depends on my attitude. I won't find the beauty of this season if I'm grumbling about it.

"But if I'm willing to receive both the good and the hard from my loving Father's hand – then He will open my eyes to see the gems He has for me when the road is rocky and hard."[6]

Sally shared two scriptures that give her strength during her husband's journey. They are both a critical reminder that this life is but a moment in eternity. We must never forget this as we fight the good fight of faith.

> *Our light and momentary troubles are achieving for us an eternal glory that far outweighs them all.*
> **2 Corinthians 4:17**

> *Friends, when life gets really difficult, don't jump to the conclusion that God isn't on the job. Instead, be glad that you are in the very thick of what Christ experienced. This is a spiritual refining process, with glory just around the corner.* **1 Peter 4:12, 13**

I believe the Kingdom warrior that will usher in the coming of Christ will be part John Wimber, Bill Johnson, and Henri Nouwen – believers who believe in the healing power of Christ, yet understand that healing in its fullness is still to come. Until then, we fight sickness and disease as Christ gives us His power to do so. Henri Nouwen beautifully writes:

"Jesus is God's wounded healer: through His wounds we are healed. Jesus' suffering and death brought joy and life. His humiliation brought glory; His rejection brought a community of love. As followers of Jesus we can also allow our wounds to bring healing to others."[7]

With all that God gives you – use for His glory.

SUPERNATURAL

POWER

I GLORY to

GOD

ESTABLISH HIS KINGDOM

SIGNS & WONDERS

motivated by
COMPASSION

MIRACLES

the
Gift
of

Chapter Eleven

Living the Power Gifts:
Do You Believe in Miracles? Yes!

The Gift of Miracles

"This is the pastor who prays for the sick," was my quick introduction to the family as they escorted me upstairs to their very sick aunt.

I've prayed for thousands, and though she looked very ill, I expected the Lord to heal when I placed my hand on her forehead.

Immediately, she exhaled, never taking another breath.

The family, realizing she had just died, did not share my calm. In my mind, this was merely an opportunity for a miracle, a resurrection from the dead.

Welcome to the world of ministry where miracles can happen or not.

I commanded life to come back into her body. I rebuked death. I bound the enemy. Nothing. My prayers grew louder and more desperate. I prayed and prayed until the family asked me to leave. They actually asked me to leave.

Welcome to the world of ministry where miracles can happen or not.

The Gift of Miracles is:[1]

a. Supernatural power to intervene and counteract earthly and evil forces

b. Literally means a display of power giving the ability to go beyond the natural

c. Operates closely with the gifts of faith and healing to bring authority over sin, Satan, sickness, and the binding forces of this age

There are few things in life like the intensity of an emergency room – the quick, purposeful movements of the staff, the whirls and clicks of machines, the tense emotions of family. I've visited quite a few over the years, seen the presence of God fill a room and healing come. But nothing like this.

The brother of one of our church members was fighting for his life. Initially considered to be dead after falling off a ladder, paramedics worked diligently to finally get a faint heartbeat.

When I entered the hospital, I could see the large group of family and friends filling the waiting room. I found this man's wife, who was of course distraught, and had begun to speak with her, when the E.R. doctor interrupted with devastating news. "We just have to tell you, he's gone. We've got a slight heartbeat, we're getting oxygen in, but he's gone. He was out too long. He'll never recover. He will be brain dead. You need to just let him go…"

She was weeping. Two small kids, now no father, yet she turned to me after the doctor left and said, "Please, will you pray?"

Of course I would. "Yes," I replied, wanting to bring any kind of comfort to her and the family – but no thoughts of healing. The doctor just gave the prognosis. What could I do?

I walked to his bedside, grayish skin tone, unresponsive, wires and machines surrounding him. I planned to put my hands on him and pray what would amount to an evangelical version of the Last Rites, "Lord, I pray he goes to heaven and I hope he knows you." Then I'd go out to the family and hopefully speak some words of solace. God had other plans.

Just as I laid my hands on him and started my obligatory prayers, I heard a voice. I've heard the Lord's voice a couple of times in the past. It's impossible to accurately describe. I wish it

sounded like Charlton Heston, but when
you hear it, you're not sure if it's actually
audible to others or so strong within
yourself that you perceive it as audible.
But it's much, much more than that still,
small voice most believers have "heard" – this was loud, strong,
and direct.

I will raise him on the third day.

"I will raise him on the third day."

We are all jars of clay. Cracked pots. How God puts up
with us, I do not know. "Lord, that sounded like you... Can
you say that again?"

And, I heard it again.

It's astonishing how fast the mind works. In a split second it
seemed like a thousand thoughts fought for attention. I was
thinking, "Wow! Raise him on the third day, how biblical."

I began a conversation with the Lord, not necessarily full of
faith. Moses or Mr. Heston would not be proud. My
monologue with God covered insurance issues, financial failure,
and my social standing.

It boiled down to this, "They're gonna think I'm nuts." I
needed another sign. I guess an audible voice from God wasn't
enough. "Lord, if that's really you... open his eyes."

The second I spoke it and pointed toward his eyes, they opened. Partially assured, I spoke under my breath, "That was a pretty good sign... I can't argue with that." Of course, then came a thousand more thoughts, most of them trying to convince me to say nothing to the family.

In the waiting room – filled, standing room only – all eyes focused on me as I entered. "This is what the Lord says, leave him for three days and in three days he will open his eyes and there will be nothing wrong."

Barely engaging anyone after my pronouncement, I left, immediately regretting my message. This accident was tragic and my words to her and the family, if not from God, cruel.

To make matters worse, I would leave the next day on a family vacation. Each day I called trying to find out this man's status. No one could seem to reach them. "Yeah, because he's done, and now I'm done." I was miserable in doubt and fear – great man of God whimpering like a scolded puppy.

A week later in a church service, still no word, but the brother of the nearly dead man raised his hand to share. He had a smile, so I had hope.

"You all know what happened to my brother. I found my brother dead." He told them the story of the accident while I waited for an eternity. "But Pastor told us on the third day he's gonna come out. So we kept him alive and we told the doctors, 'No, you keep him for three days like our pastor said. You keep him for three days!'"

Eternity just got longer.

"On the third day he sat up in his bed. Just sat up. Nothing was wrong. And the first thing he said to everyone, 'I need to go back to church.'"

Everyone in the waiting room, some 45 people, started to attend our church. On the last day as pastors of this church, before we became missionaries, the very last person to say a heartfelt goodbye was this man, a very grateful husband and father of two.

Raising from the Dead

Miracles in the Bible and miracles today have the same purpose: One, to bring glory to God and to establish the Kingdom of God; two, to bless the person(s) receiving the miracle; three, to serve as a catalyst to those impacted by the miracle to repent and give their lives to God – AND be a witness to others.

The following is a story as experienced by two people I know and respect. Pastors William and Christina Yakumba from Papua New Guinea left their home for Kiribati in 2009.

Kiribati is part of a cluster of small picturesque tropical islands spread across the South Pacific with a population of some 60,000 inhabitants.

That year, William and Christina established the first Foursquare church in a rental house with two young people. They faithfully shared the gospel and served the needs of the people. However, few people responded to their message. Witchcraft dominated the island ways.

That all changed one afternoon.

"My mummy, my mummy is dead!" were the screams heard in the local dialect from a teenage girl running toward her pastor's house.

Pastor William and Christina walked back to the home of this mother who had collapsed and died. With no electricity or telephones and the medical center six miles away, options were limited. But faith rose in each of these servants as they walked, consoling a distraught daughter and praying along the way.

This teenager had shown great courage by joining the new church and by running to her pastors. Word of the mother's death had spread rapidly and instead of showing support, neighbors formed a gauntlet of abuse and insults.

Entering the dead mother's house, no walls, only woven coconut mats for privacy, William and Christina went directly to the body covered by a white sheet. Mourners filled the house with wailing. None of those in the house, including the deceased, were believers, only the teenage girl.

William was uneasy in the room full of skeptical people, yet he knew without doubt he would pray for this woman to be raised back to life. Moving in the gift of wisdom, he gathered the immediate family together and shared the story of Jesus praying for his friend, Lazarus. He then instructed the family to hold hands and join him in prayer.

Then, William knelt beside the body, laying his hands on her body. Christina prayed with the family. Together they rebuked death, commanding life to come back into her body.

Powerful prayers, but nothing happened.

William opened his Bible and read John 10:10,

> *The thief does not come except to steal, and to kill and to destroy. I have come that they may have life, and that they may have it more abundantly.*

Ten more minutes passed. People in the house, especially those closest to the body, became agitated. Some jumped up, running out of the house. No one noticed the slight twitching in the fingers of the corpse. That changed quickly when her movement became unmistakable. Steadily, she recovered completely, being joined on the floor with her husband and children, sipping a simple glass of water.

Pastor William gathered the people together to share the Scripture and many received Christ as their Savior. Eventually, a revival took place with many of those who witnessed the resurrection from the dead being evangelists, giving a powerful and indisputable message:

"She who was once dead is now alive."

The church grew exponentially. Evangelical crusades took place throughout the island. Healing and deliverance continue to this day along with a healthy mother and grateful daughter.

3 in One

As mentioned before, the gifts of the Spirit often work in concert. Here is a story from my friend Greg Biddell, a fellow author and healing practitioner.

> "I was ministering throughout the nation of Kenya and while on my way to an open-air revival meeting we passed through the local markets. Kenyan markets are filled with the crush of thousands.

"In the service we saw the Holy Spirit move with the gift of knowledge and about a dozen sick people healed. I then spoke out and said, 'There is a lady here today who has breast cancer and if you come now, Jesus will heal you.' The problem was, there was no response and I thought that being in a foreign country this could be an embarrassment to the woman; so we closed the service.

"About 10 or 15 minutes later, and as everyone was leaving, I saw this one lady walking toward me. She asked, 'Are you the man who said Jesus will heal me of breast cancer?' I answered, 'Yes.' But, I was intrigued as to why it had taken her so long to respond to the call of the Lord.

"Her explanation was she hadn't attended the open-air meeting as she was buying her food from the markets down the road. She told me that when I spoke out those words she heard them and started walking immediately.

"The wonderful thing about this testimony is the Lord used me in the gift of the word of knowledge and then he sent his word a distance of several miles to the lady with cancer, which was a miracle. And, of course, there was the gift of healing because the woman was made whole."

The following miracle story comes from good friend Dr. Leslie Keegel and his outstanding book *The Spirit of the Lord is Upon Us.*

"The wood ladder protested with every step up its weathered rungs until I reached the roof of an equally old house. My view was muted by the gray Bulgarian sky that hung like a wet canopy over the gathering people below. I began to pray.

I always expect God to move in power. The Kingdom of God rarely takes territory from the Kingdom of Darkness in quiet.

"Billed as the 'Indian Preacher,' which I thought a reference to my dark skin and South Asian features, the people were initially disappointed. They somehow expected an American Indian dressed in full native regalia, probably hoping for a bit of America's 'Old West' experience, or at least the Hollywood version. I learned later that my skin color, similar to theirs, would suffice.

"I began my sermon from this most unusual pulpit with a usual message – Jesus saves and Jesus heals. It was shorter than most, even with the translation. I finished by asking the crowd, now over a thousand, to respond to the gospel.

"I always expect God to move in power. The Kingdom of God rarely takes territory from the Kingdom of Darkness in quiet. I may not always see the results at the altar, but I believe the same Jesus who felt compassion for the lost and sick always arrives on time.

"It didn't take long for him to make an introduction to this community of Gypsies. I imagine this group, used to poverty and prejudice, reminded Jesus of his own people two thousand years ago.

"And I got to watch it all from the rooftop.

"One person, then two, then another lifted their bodies from makeshift wheelchairs, taking short steps that backed away the tightly packed crowd.

"The cries that came from healing joined the whispers of astonishment. People screamed, people fell, hands were raised, and heads were bowed. It was as if Jesus walked through the crowd touching all he saw the Father touching.

"I wanted to join the people, but my host demanded that I stay on the roof, fearing the crowd would crush me. My eye caught the sight of a young woman holding a baby. She held her infant with her healthy arm, but the other was deformed – it had stopped growing at the elbow with what looked like fingers protruding out.

"I scanned across the horizon full of people being touched by the power of God, but was drawn back to the woman with the deformed arm. She had fallen under the weight of the glory of God. To this day, I don't know if she screamed in fear or if there was pain involved. But what happened next would nearly cause a panic in the crowd of people who watched.

"Her deformed arm began to grow – I only wished I could have been closer to describe it more accurately. In a matter of minutes, God had restored to her a perfectly formed arm with perfectly functioning fingers.

"Still, my Bulgarian host would not let me go down from the roof until all the people had gone. I watched, I wept, I prayed. When I finally descended the ladder, dozens of gypsy children, holding freshly picked wild flowers, came running toward me – their faces full of joy and wonder. I was the one who had brought the message and received their grateful gifts; but the truth was that I simply proclaimed the gospel and Jesus confirmed it in power."[2]

More On the Gift of Miracles

Jesus' miracles were often motivated by compassion. This is a primary reason, I believe, that compassion-type ministries should be involved in the Gifts, especially miracles. But, for some reason, the Church tends to continue separating the two, when in fact, Jesus did not. Even His walking on water was motivated out of compassion for His terrified disciples, or changing water to wine to help His mother solve a crisis at a wedding.

Compassion ministries, whether expressed by the local church or parachurch, extend the hands and heart of God to His people. How much more evangelistically effective could they be if compassion was cloaked in power?

The death and resurrection of Lazarus (John 11) captures both the compassionate and confirmative nature of a miracle. Jesus was moved by Lazarus' grieving family and by the loss of a friend, but there was an even higher purpose: to confirm His divinity.

The Texas Compassion Moment

Obviously, miracles leave a lifelong impact – not only on the beneficiary of the miracle, but also on the one believing for the miracle. In fact, such a divine intervention by God may change the trajectory of one's career.

John Rusk, newly saved during the powerful "Jesus Movement" believed that the power of God and evangelism worked well together. He would often go out with a couple of his friends into the parks of small Texas towns. This small team of young people would often approach drug addicts and homeless in the public square and ask if they could pray for them. Often times they asked to pray for legs to be lengthened, something they had faith for and had seen frequently. Even John's father experienced such a healing, curing him completely from chronic back pain. "We were kind of a divine chiropractic prayer team," John would later joke.

One evening, in another small Texas town that bordered Mexico, John and his team asked those in the square, "Hey, want to see a miracle?" They asked the question both to draw attention of others and to pray for someone's legs to lengthen. They didn't expect the response.

"Well, do you think God can do that for me?" The voice came from behind John. Without looking at the man, John said, "Yes, of course He can!"

When John turned around and saw this man, his heart went up to his throat. The gentleman who stood before him possessed only a four-inch stub where an arm should have been, with curled up fingers coming out of the deformed appendage.

> He had barely prayed, "Thank you, Jesus," when in John's words, "a new arm exploded out of his body."

But, John heard encouragement from the Lord and instructed this man to stick out his deformed arm. He had barely prayed, "Thank you, Jesus," when in John's words, "a new arm exploded out of his body."

By then, a small crowd had gathered and witnessed this extraordinary event. People gasped and screamed. Some fainted. One young Catholic girl fell under the power of the Spirit, speaking in tongues. A mini-revival ensued, seeing other miracles and healings, including several people walking out of wheelchairs.

This event, this miracle, set the course for young John Rusk's life, leading him into full-time ministry, much as a missionary in

Africa. There he continued to see the power and compassion of God working together, bringing thousands to Christ.

When it All Comes Together – Even When You Have No Faith

God is in charge. He is sovereign. He, however, decided to work through "earthen vessels," a.k.a. cracked pots, like you and me. Perfect God + fallen human = sometimes messy, but always as He wills.

Nothing gives me more assurance of God's complete control in the area of His Gifts as when I hear a story from some fellow "leaky vessel" who describes how God moved – despite themself.

Nothing gives me more assurance of God's complete control in the area of His Gifts as when I hear a story from some fellow "leaky vessel" who describes how God moved – despite themself. I love the humility, but even more, the stark realization and appropriation of the words of Jesus to His disciples:

Apart from me you can do nothing. John 15:5

Recently, I listened intently to a story from someone I implicitly trust. We sat in my living room, I taking copious notes, while Greg Fisher told the following story, with his usual self-effacing humor and humility. Greg and his wife, Margaret, served many effective years as missionaries in Africa.

The Dead Leg

"'I'll have two days to finally kick back and rest,' I thought. My travel schedule had been brutal up to that point. Exhausted, I still had duties in a little town in Ghana I was visiting, but nothing overwhelming, until I was 'discovered' by an African evangelist who also happened to be in town. It's hard to say 'no' to someone who is so insistent – so we got in our 4-wheel-drive and drove over some rough roads to a village he demanded we visit.

"Upon arriving, normally you'd stop first at the village chief's 'palace,' but we passed him by and drove directly to a typically small house. Entering this humble home, I noticed two older, stoic women on the bed and a younger woman lying on a mat in the middle of the room.

"This young woman's left leg, twice the size of the other leg and much darker in color. It was bad; but as a missionary in Africa, I was used to bad. We immediately prayed, and prayed, and prayed. We laid on hands, prayed some more, but nothing visually happened.

"Then this evangelist pronounced to the few who had gathered in the room, 'And now, our missionary is going to pray!'

"I had been praying up to that point; but I guess he wanted to make it official with a formal announcement – that, or he was stalling for time hoping something would happen to build our waning faith.

"So, I prayed some more. I prayed louder. I quoted scriptures. I think I even made up a few scriptures. I threw out an everything-I-know-kitchen-sink prayer. It's amazing how we filibuster in prayer when we have no faith.

"Then, thankfully, God stepped in. I blurted out a word of knowledge. 'This is not a physical disease, this is a curse!' The best I can describe it, at that exact moment, the room got electric. The atmosphere changed. Then I pronounced, 'We are going to break this curse today!'

"I instructed us all to begin to worship and to sing songs that elevated the Lordship of Jesus Christ. The presence of God came into that very desperate room. Then I commanded in the name of Jesus for the curse to be broken. Nothing physical happened, but I sensed something occurring in the spirit.

"Satisfied that I did all I could, we packed up the car to leave, when the evangelist insisted we take the afflicted woman with us. The village came out in force, shouting to her as she limped toward our vehicle. I later would learn they were yelling, 'Don't go! The white people will cut off your leg!'

"After returning to the small town, I fulfilled my duties in the next couple of days and planned to return to my home. I told a young American missionary wannabe, who had been traveling with me, that we'd stop to see this young lady.

"Entering her room, we were greeted by the all too familiar odor: Gangrene. Her leg was no longer dying; it was dead. I prayed for her, more as an exit strategy than with any faith. In the car, this young missionary-to-be asked the innocent question, 'Was there anything else we could have done?'

"'Like what?' I'm sure my tart retort conveyed my annoyance. 'Like take her to a hospital?' my answer even more caustic. 'Did you see a hospital? There's not even a doctor for miles.' And then I shared the stark but common reality for so many sick in developing nations. 'Unless God heals her, she's going to die.'

"Two months later, the evangelist came to my home. After 15 minutes of traditional Ghanaian greetings, I asked the question, 'What ever happened to the lady with the leg?'

"'Oh, yes,' he replied. 'You didn't know the whole story.' He had my attention. 'Remember the two older ladies on the bed?' I nodded in acknowledgment. 'They were her aunties. And they had a curse put on her.'

"This fact didn't surprise me. It was common for people in the region to put curses on someone in the village who they felt was doing too well. A kind of spiritual socialism – get too far above the rest of us and we'll put you back in your place. In this case, the aunties had hired the most powerful priest, witchdoctor, in town. When they saw how bad she was suffering, they had called him back to reverse the curse. In fact, they were hiding some of the priest's 'instruments' under the very bed they were sitting on, thinking he might come the very day I arrived. He never did come back until something extraordinary happened.

"After I prayed my rather faithless 'exit' prayer, before we left to return home, that night she discovered she could walk. By the next day, her leg totally healed. When I left her less than 48 hours before, her leg was dead, but now alive – a true miracle. In fact, on the day of the healing, she walked back to her town, some five miles. As she strolled normally into the entrance of her village, she began proclaiming over and over, 'Jesus healed me! Jesus healed me!'

"The story gets better, but not for the cursing priest. Upon hearing that missionaries had prayed for her and his curse had been broken, he demanded money. He insisted on what amounted to years worth of wages from the poor family. He would either receive payment or place another, more powerful, curse on the entire family.

"On the day he planned to collect payment, he turned to his apprentice and complained of pain in his leg. Abruptly, and without any other signs, he dropped dead, much to the relief of the startled family.

"After this event, word got out to the entire town, 'Don't mess with the Foursquare guys; those guys have the real God!' And, of course, the church grew."

Greg's story is a wonderful reminder that God will work the miraculous through, or even despite, your weakness. In Greg's situation, he lacked faith until God gifted him with it. He lacked wisdom until God blessed him with it and they worshiped with songs of Jesus' lordship. He lacked direction until God graced him with a word of knowledge and a curse was broken. This story also shows how the Gifts often work seamlessly together – a supernatural flow, if you will.

But also, and maybe most importantly, what is required of us "cracked pots" is that we be obedient. Greg, by his own admission, didn't "feel it," but he knew, intimately, the God he served. He knew God can and

> Our ability to minister is not based on how we feel, but on how the Spirit feels for the needy.

will heal. Greg's emotions were inconsequential; what mattered is that he be obedient and pray and listen to what the Spirit of God was saying.

If we will learn this lesson, our lives will never be the same and great adventure awaits.

"Our ability to minister is not based on how we feel, but on how the Spirit feels for the needy."[3]

The Purpose of Miracles

Miracles are signs that point to God. The word *miracles* is often juxtaposed synonymously with the phrase "signs and wonders."

Miracles, signs, and wonders all give attention and glory to the maker of those very trans-natural interventions.

In the early Church, miracles were perceived as being more of a common occurrence with the purpose of establishing the validity of the message and the messenger. They were evidence that the Kingdom was being established and that heaven had invaded earth. Peter's sermon on Pentecost establishes the link between the miraculous and the authority of Christ.

Men of Israel, hear these words: Jesus of Nazareth, a Man attested by God to you by miracles, wonders, and signs which God did through Him in your midst, as you yourselves also know. Acts 2:22

Further on in Acts, persecution of believers was also becoming all too common. After being released by the chief priests, the prayer for boldness was accompanied by these words:

...by stretching out Your hand to heal, and that signs and wonders

Should today's Church operate any differently than the early Church in regard to dependence upon the Holy Spirit for boldness and signs and wonders to follow?

may be done through the name of Your holy Servant Jesus. Acts 4:30

Miracles meant the Lordship, the divinity of Jesus would be established and the body of Christ, the Church, would grow.

And with great power (dunamis) *the apostles gave witness to the resurrection of the Lord Jesus.* Acts 4:33

Should today's Church operate any differently than the early Church in regard to dependence upon the Holy Spirit for boldness and signs and wonders to follow?

Of course, that is a question debated over the centuries and a question muted in large part by the lack of power exhibited only sporadically up until the Azusa Street Revival.

The answer to the question should be biblically based, applying all proper hermeneutics, and the answer would be a resounding "No."

The problem for many Western churches is a continuation of a model that makes miracles and the other gifts as rare exceptions, not normative to the daily life of the church.

Having ministered on all the continents, save Antarctica, I can report that the churches of non-Western nations typically possess an orthodoxy and orthopraxy that fully embrace a

Christianity that is gift-filled and Spirit-led. And that includes the non-Pentecostal, more traditional church.

This is because the typical non-Western believer has experienced what the late Dr. Paul Hiebert refers to as the "excluded middle"[4] even before conversion. This middle experience, or a part of daily life, involves spirits, good and bad, and supernatural events that challenge the empirical mind.

> As the non-Western church leads the way, miracles fulfill their purpose and millions become followers of Jesus Christ.

Is there any correlation between this paradigm and the exponential growth of the church in Africa, Latin America, and even Asia? I believe there is. And I further believe Europe and the States are ripe for revival. However, our leaders must cast off the old paradigm that church is a non-participatory, passive experience.

As the non-Western church leads the way, miracles fulfill their purpose and millions become followers of Jesus Christ.

Position Yourself to See

Is our life one in which we expect miracles? Most believers today would probably say no, especially those who live in developed nations. The problem, in part, is that we in the West are trained to see life as a series of random chances, not the daily moving of the hand of God. We compartmentalize life in general – our work life, family life, school life, etc. We tend to see God and the things of God as one of those compartments.

The early Church did not. God was the epicenter of their lives – nothing else came close.

A very successful businessperson and good personal friend, Winnie Long, refuses to see life exclusively through an empirical prism. In fact, she wrote a book describing her worldview, *Miracles Unaware*.[5] This title aptly describes her lifestyle of seeing God in everything and everyone. Miracles may come in small packages, but they come more often than we imagine, she teaches. Once we begin to live life expecting the small interventions of God, expecting the big miracles is not such the great leap.

The first church operated under such a paradigm; they saw from the Day of Pentecost the hand of God and never looked back. To position ourselves for miracles we must begin by believing that God is there, everywhere, everyday, every hour, and sometimes we must merely open our eyes to see.

The world that we are charged to win for Christ is not interested in a God that only lives in one of your compartments. They must see He is alive and well and living in you.

PROPHECY

THE GIFT OF

divinely anointed utterance

REVELATION

RESTORATION

IMPARTATION

EDIFICATION

EXHORTATION

Does it build up, encourage or comfort?

Chapter Twelve

Living the Inspirational Gifts: Thus Said the Lord

The Gift of Prophecy

Was he a man or was he an angel? Either way, he brought a life-changing word from the Lord.

"Ministry at the Sepulveda Foursquare Church wasn't working and I didn't see any reason to keep trying, I just wanted out. I decided it was time to resign. I didn't want anyone telling me that I should hang on any longer. I didn't even want to talk to God about it, except to occasionally yell and complain about how unfair this was. You know what I mean; we have all been there. I certainly didn't want to talk to my wife, Bev, about it because I knew what her response would be and I didn't want to hear it. I quietly wrote my letter of resignation and planned to give it to the church elders at our meeting that night.

"Because space was extremely limited, the elders met in a small circle at the front of our little church sanctuary. With my letter of resignation in hand, we began the meeting with prayer. As we started to pray, the double doors of the little sanctuary opened, and in walked a big African American man. I had never seen him before. He was not the kind of man you would easily forget. He was built like an American football player but dressed in a light colored, three-pieced suit. Immediately, I stood up to go let him know that this was not a public meeting. I had a strange feeling as I approached him that only increased when he said, 'Hi, Dan.' How did he know my name? I was sure I'd never seen him before.

"I asked if we had met and his response only added to the already strange feeling, 'Yes, we have, but not quite like this.' What kind of answer was that? Of course, I had to ask again, 'Have we met before?' He quickly responded, 'That's not important! What is important now is that I have a message from Father: Don't give up. Don't quit. It's small now, but it will grow!'

"I was shocked! I didn't know what to say. Everything in me wanted to reach out and touch him, but I couldn't. 'Who are you?' I asked again. He repeated, 'Don't give up. Don't quit. It's small now, but it will grow!' By this time, the elders who had only heard part of what he was saying stood up and began to walk toward us.

"As they approached, he opened the double doors leading into the lobby area and out the front door he went. We were only a few feet behind him, but as we followed him out the front doors, he was gone. We looked everywhere; there was no way he could have gotten away without us seeing it. We were right there! I have no question in my mind that we encountered an angel sent from God to deliver a message to this young pastor who was ready to give it all up and walk out in deep shame and disappointment.

"Needless to say, I didn't go ahead with my plan to resign that night. When the shock wore off, I showed the elders my letter and told the story. None of us questioned that we came face to face with an angel that night. When I think back over the years of ministry, I wouldn't change the time we spent at the little green church on Orion Street for anything."[1]

> Prophecy, when exercised properly, brings a dynamic to the church and to its members.

My good friend Dan Sneed's story of a prophetic encounter that altered his ministry and life reminds us of the power in hearing words that came from the heart of God. Prophecy, when exercised properly, brings a dynamic to the church and to its members.

What is the Gift of Prophecy?

The Gift of Prophecy as defined by the late church growth expert C. Peter Wagner:

"The gift of prophecy is the special ability that God gives to members of the Body of Christ to receive and communicate an immediate message of God to his people through a divinely anointed utterance."[2]

Prophecy, in both the Old and New Testaments, fulfills two needs: *foretelling* which is speaking about events to come in the future, and *forthtelling* which communicates a specific message from the heart of God.

According to Paul in 1 Corinthians 14:31,

For you can all prophesy one by one, that all may learn and all may be encouraged.

Yet, he recognizes the ministry of the prophet in Ephesians 4:11,

Though all can prophesy not all are prophets.

Prophecy and You

And he himself gave some to be apostles, some prophets, some evangelists, and some pastors and teachers.

Ephesians 4:11

And God has appointed these in the church: first apostles, second prophets, third teachers, after that miracles, then gifts of healings, helps, administrations, varieties of tongues. **1 Corinthians 12:28**

Misunderstanding the ministry of the prophet from the gift of prophecy is a root of some confusion in the church today. Simply stated, all of us can prophesy, but not all of us operate in the ministry of the prophet. They move consistently in this gift and are recognized by the church for their character and accuracy.

Typically this ministry of the prophet does four things:

1. They bring revelation. They speak about things that are hidden.

2. They bring restoration. Restoration means they build up that which has been torn down.

3. They bring impartation. A prophet activates the gifts of God in believers.

4. They bring understanding. A real prophetic voice will give a true understanding of the Word of God.

As Paul states in 1 Corinthians 12:29, "Are all prophets?" The answer is no. Yet, in chapter 14 verse 1 he encourages all to "Pursue love and desire spiritual gifts, but especially that you may prophesy."

It is important to note the shift in the Old Covenant of a few prophets to the New where all are empowered to prophesy. Dr. Steve Schell notes:

"This shift from a few to all is an essential element in Joel (see Acts 2:17, 18) about God's restoration of His people in the last days."

Dr. Schell adds:

"He sent the Holy Spirit to dwell inside every man, woman and child who was willing to repent and believe in Him (Acts 2:38, 39). From that moment on, not only could all prophesy, all could do every type of ministry that Jesus had done (John 14:12).[3]

Pursue prophecy. Possibly in that pursuit you will discover that God has chosen you to operate in the ministry of a prophet.

Yet, many have misunderstood and have concluded that after using this gift it puts them automatically in the category of the ministry of prophet. It does not. Those spiritually mature, especially your pastor and other leaders in the church, will either recognize that divine appointment or not.

Pastor and author Ben Dixon summarizes it well,

"…not only can EVERYONE hear the voice of God personally (John 10:27), but EVERYONE can hear the voice of God prophetically as well."[4]

Its Purpose

Edification, Exhortation, and Comfort

According to 1 Corinthians 14:3,

> *But he who prophesies speaks edification and exhortation and comfort to men.*

How?

Edification – to build something up, to strengthen

Paul considered prophecy extremely important because of its power to build up the Body of Christ.

Exhortation – to push forward, to encourage forward

To comfort – rather self-explanatory. A word which brings one a sense of comfort.

So, when someone has a prophetic word for you, ask yourself three things: Does it build me up? Does it encourage me? (Does it push me forward?) Or does it bring me comfort?

I remember a young man, the son of a pastor, who walked away from God due in large part to a "word" that did not fit the above parameters and was not of God.

During a Sunday service a woman stood up and proclaimed with all the emotions and religious verbiage, "Yea, even verily," while pointing to this young man, "thou art the black sheep of the family." And not content to merely humiliate, she concluded, "And thou shalt surely die."

Not good. Unfortunately, the flesh produces death. Fortunately, I was able to see this young man restored years later.

Jerry Cook says it well:

"To live prophetically in the world means to speak Christ's love and redemptive power into

> While building up a believer's faith and giving deeper understanding, prophecy has the ability to reveal the intentions of the heart – causing a deep and real repentance.

the heart of individuals caught in sin. We see Jesus doing this…He touched this sick person, he released that demon-possessed person, he forgave the other person who was a notorious sinner."[5]

It also serves as a sign to unbelievers that what they are hearing is from God.

While building up a believer's faith and giving deeper understanding, prophecy has the ability to reveal the intentions of the heart – causing a deep and real repentance.

But if all prophesy, and an unbeliever or an uninformed person comes in, he is convinced by all, he is convicted by all. And thus the secrets of his heart are revealed; and so, falling down on his face, he will worship God and report that God is truly among you. 1 Corinthians 14:24-25

There is also place for prophetic words that tell what will happen in the future and to be a warning. (See John 16:13; Acts 11:28; Acts 21:10-11; Revelation 1:10)

However, most prophecy exercised today is not a prediction, but more of a present day word from God.

According to theologian Wayne Grudem, prophecy is "telling something that God has spontaneously brought to mind."[6]

It's critical to understand that any prophetic word does not give any new revelation into who God is – that is all in the Bible. Prophecy can, however, illuminate the Word of God allowing it to "come alive" to the hearer, even personalizing it to the person receiving it.

> Sharing an accurate prophetic word or a word of knowledge or wisdom all depends on one thing: how to hear from God.

And, prophetic words should never have the level of honor that the Bible does. The Bible is God's written word. A prophecy, in its essence, according to Mike Bickle:

> "conveys to our mind thoughts that we imperfectly communicate with our words."[7]

Because we are imperfect humans hearing words from God, we must move in all humility.

The Key to Moving in the Prophetic Word: Hearing God's Voice

Sharing an accurate prophetic word or a word of knowledge or wisdom all depends on one thing: how to hear from God.

My sheep hear my voice, and I know them, and they follow me. **John 10:27**

God wants to speak to you. Wouldn't your earthly father want to both hear from you and speak to you? Why not your Heavenly Father?

> *However, when He, the Spirit of truth, has come, He will guide you into all truth; for He will not speak on His own authority, but whatever He hears He will speak; and He will tell you things to come.* John 16:13

How Does He Speak?

More wisdom from Dr. Steve Schell:

"Most believers need to be taught that we can prophesy. The thought of speaking the word of the Lord can be so intimidating that we can be afraid to step out and try. And, frankly, few of us know anyone who is able to teach us how. So, when we read these passages in the Bible about the gifts of the Spirit we acknowledge that they are true, but we have a hard time acknowledging that they are true for us. We don't know where to start. We think to ourselves, 'Maybe the Spirit will come upon me so strongly someday that I will helplessly blurt out a word that God wants me to say. But until then, I don't want to say anything because I might say something wrong.' That attitude of caution is certainly better than being willing to speak whether the word came from God or not. But our only options aren't silence or recklessness. There is a way to learn how to prophesy, and in a healthy church there will be people who know Scripture soundly enough to help us evaluate what we are hearing (1 Corinthians 14:29). So, if we're brave enough to try and humble enough to be corrected, we will, in time, learn to recognize the source of what we're hearing, and be able to test for ourselves whether a word is in agreement with Scripture. Then, with practice, we can let God speak through us whenever He wants to."[8]

Remember – perfect God, imperfect human. God has many ways to convey to you His heart. Always be humble. Here's an incomplete list:

- Impressions in your mind – The still small voice

- An overwhelming sense in your mind and emotions

- A scripture that comes to mind, often with an application

- A word or phrase, images, pictures

- Dreams, visions – In the Muslim world, thousands of testimonies have come forward of people seeing and communicating with Jesus.

- Through an individual who may or may not know you

- Even a book or a video – The Lord has often led me to specific books that contained exactly the message I needed from God.

- A teaching from your church – How many times have you sat there in amazement after hearing a teaching you know was just for you?

- An audible voice – There are rare reports from respected believers of hearing an actual disembodied voice. Three times I have heard the Lord audibly speak to me.

- Through songs, even poetry

The key is to be open, then step out in faith – learning as you move in humility and love.

> *I say to myself, I will not mention Him, I will speak in His name no more. But then it becomes like a fire burning in my heart, imprisoned in my bones.* Jeremiah 20:9

It's All in the Delivery

Remember the story of Papa Jones speaking a "prophetic word" in the midst of great people of faith?

"Thus saith the Lord God of Israel!"

For many years in many Pentecostal circles, prophetic utterances seemed to be as much about the delivery as the actual words – and sometimes style over substance.

What made Papa Jones' "word" so special was the humility in which he ended it, "Flesh, flesh, flesh!" Something much greater than impressing his fellow man motivated Brother Jones: impressing his God.

We all should be so humble – humility based on a sincere fear of the Lord. Such godly reverence is the foundation of all prophetic words.

But, what about the delivery?

I believe there is room for a variety of the Lord's leading when it comes to a delivery and introduction of a prophetic word. As I mentioned before, in some cultures a more relaxed, relational "I'm sensing" would not be as well

If you are a person who hates to be wrong, prophecy might not be for you.

received as a "Thus says the Lord." What's important is to hear God's voice and deliver it in a way it can best be received – all so that God is glorified.

Dare to be Wrong

If you are a person who hates to be wrong, prophecy might not be for you. Hearing from God is, at best, an imprecise art. We see through a "glass dimly," the Apostle Paul reminds us. Because of our sin nature, we at times will not hear clearly, completely, or even at all – flesh, flesh, flesh.

If you are someone who is not open to falling down and getting up again and again, this might be a difficult gift for you. Yet, personally and among those I most admire and respect in the prophetic world, we all grow each time we are willing to be used by God. Each time there is no guarantee that you won't hear wrong or at least incompletely. But you can guarantee that the Lord will be patient, kind, and desiring for you to succeed. He does not want you to be humiliated nor does He want His body to be damaged. His mercies are tender every morning, so be courageous!

More Moving in the Prophetic[9]

- As in the use of all the Gifts, moving in the prophetic should be motivated by love.
  (1 Corinthians 14:1)

- Believers should desire to move in this gift.
  (1 Corinthians 14:1, 39)

- In a public church setting, prophetic words should be limited to two or three at any one time.
  (1 Corinthians 14:29)

- Prophetic words may come from Scripture, visions (see Acts 18:9), dreams (Matthew 2:13), impressions, an audible voice from God.

- Prophecy most likely will occur in an atmosphere of prayer and worship. (Acts 13:2)

- The person prophesying should be in full emotional control (1 Corinthians 14:32) not given to "ranting."

- Can be short (Haggai 1:13 "I am with you.")

Why the Prophetic is So Important TODAY

The darker the world becomes, the brighter the light needs to shine. God is raising up an army of believers who will be His voice. To do so properly, they must be in a position to hear, then speak, then love.

This is especially true of the younger generation, hungry not for man's voice, but to hear from God. That is why our teaching from the Bible must be done with Spirit-led clarity and driven by Spirit-filled purpose. The church must be open to the office of the prophet, but also to exercising and encouraging the gift of prophecy among all believers.

Again from Ben Dixon,

"What would it look like if every church had a healthy prophetic ministry? As I travel from church to church, I think about this very question. Most places seek to have sound teaching, passionate worship, strong leadership, and a compelling vision. However, I have not seen many churches that are developing a healthy and fruitful prophetic ministry."[10]

Joel's prophecy is as true today as it was during the Day of Pentecost.

In those days I will pour out my Spirit even on my servants – men and women alike – and they will prophesy. **Acts 2:18**

The prophetic word unleashed will revive "dead bones."[11] (see Ezekiel 37:1-14)

Then he said to me, "Speak a prophetic message to these bones and say, 'Dry bones, listen to the word of the LORD! This is what the Sovereign LORD says: Look! I am going to put breath into you and make you live again! I will put flesh and muscles on you and cover you with skin. I will put breath into you, and you will come to life. Then you will know that I am the LORD.'" **Ezekiel 37:4-6**

The prophetic word, as in Ezekiel's time, puts life in church and in your personal life. It takes us from hanging on till the rapture to knocking down doors of the devil. God comes alive to you. (He never has changed, but your perception does.) You receive a new reality – God is speaking.

> Sometimes the most prophetic thing you can speak is the phrase, "God loves you."

The world is hungry to hear.

Again, the Gifts are given to you to share with others. You are called to be a disciple and disciples go where the Master calls them. Disciples hear what the Master is saying. It's actually not too complicated.

I'll close this chapter with a true and very personal story.

Sometimes the most prophetic thing you can speak is the phrase, "God loves you." When it is shared in obedience to what the Holy Spirit is telling you, few words are more powerful.

One of the most difficult ministry times in my life occurred in a hospice room occupied by a bed-ridden dying man named Bob. Though I was initially discouraged from entering his room by the staff, partially due to the extreme heat he needed to stay warm and his unwillingness to talk to anyone, I visited him anyway.

Bob, as I would discover over time, once rode with a gang of bikers. I never would have guessed it by looking at him. His frame consisted of skin wrapped loosely upon bone, marked with sores that antagonized him daily.

I talked to Bob, hoping he was listening. I came to his hothouse of a room every week, sat on the side of his bed, and just spoke of things that came to my mind – things about life, regret, forgiveness, God. There is something about conversing with a dying man that made words hold more meaning.

Pending death can also intimidate. I found myself overcome and allowing this spirit to win the day. Its sting started to reach into my soul.

So I did the only thing I knew to do: I worshiped. Asking my friend, a worship leader, to come, we began to break through layers of what I can only call death. This form of spirit hovered like a thick blanket of fog you try to chase away with flailing arms.

But worship, true worship, invites the presence of God. And where the presence of the Lord is, there is freedom (2 Corinthians 3:17). This freedom opened a portal to heaven. It allowed me to have "ears to hear what the Spirit is saying."

"Bob, God loves you."

I had his attention, but it was God calling. He wanted to speak life to the dead bones.

Bob clung to the life once lived, the life where he bullied and intimidated others into submission. He desperately wanted to be in control, but his circumstances wore through the veneer.

"You have no idea what I've done," his voice weak, but words delivered in such a way to push back. My mind, like a bad horror film, flashed with a subliminal series of images of horrific, unspeakable sins.

I was taken back, but gained composure enough to reply, "Bob, God loves you. There are no sins that can keep you from that love if you ask Him to forgive you." I wish I could write that at that moment he repented. Instead, he merely turned on his side, away from me, to end the conversation.

I, however, knew the battle had just begun. Warring in the Spirit is hard. Anyone who tells you otherwise probably has never been in its trenches.

In the next few weeks, Bob became weaker, going in and out of the comatose state that would usher him into eternity. Often, I would hold his hand, repeating scriptures, the wonderful plan of salvation, and the words that I believe stirred even his deadened soul.

"God loves you."

On my last visit before he died, I again held his hand. I again repeated those words that I believed were prophetically given. And I asked Bob, after praying the prayer of salvation, that if he believed what I was praying to squeeze my hand.

However faint, I felt his hand tighten around mine. I look forward to one day seeing Bob on the other side.

One word from God is worth more than a thousand from man. I don't know where I heard this, but I believe it with all my heart.

The generation that will usher in His Coming will be speaking words from the heart of God. Until that day, young and old must remain faithful to hear, speak, and love.

INSPIRED by Holy the Spirit

PRAY

The Gift of
TONGUES

Comfort & Interpretation

Public Worship

EDIFY

with the

S
P
I
R
I
T

Private Prayer

BATTLE in the SPIRIT

"I thank God that I speak in tongues..."

Chapter Thirteen

Living the Inspirational Gifts: To Speak or Not to Speak

The Gift of Tongues and the Gift of Interpretation

"Oh no, not again."

I said this to myself as the Bible study leader, a dear friend and mentor of mine, invited people to be prayed for to receive their prayer language.

OK, Lord, if you want me to speak in tongues, have someone tap me on the shoulder.

Praying for tongues became a vocation. For years I sought this gift. For years I was disappointed. At one church they actually tried to "teach me" to speak in tongues, putting different syllabic combinations on a chalkboard. No thanks. As much as I believed in this gift, I would never fake it or force it.

I reached a point, more emotionally than spiritually, when I could no longer seek the gift. In layman's terms, I was done. But, the desire still existed within me. Almost as if to make it harder for God, I prayed as the leader gave the last call, "OK, Lord, if you want me to speak in tongues, have someone tap me on the shoulder." Just to add to the drama, "But this is the last time."

Of course the Bible study leader extended the invitation to be prayed for, but I felt secure in my corner of the room, away from the crowd, just in case someone might inadvertently touch me on my shoulder.

When I felt the tap gently touch my shoulder, immediately I looked around, but nobody was near. It gave me just enough faith to stand up and walk to the front for one last prayer to receive. Still determined to not fake it, the few syllables that I had not predetermined spilled from my mouth with an easy flow as my mentor laid hands on me.

The moment lacked the intensity of emotion I had expected, but instead a calm, peaceful state came over me as I repeated these new (to me) syllables or words I'd never heard before.

In a sense, I had been "blind" to another dimension of the Spirit. After the laying on of hands, an impartation took place that would change my life forever. That teacher, my friend and mentor, Dr. Jerry Wheeler, lovingly laid his hands on me and without any dramatics or pressure calmly trusted the Holy Spirit to do that which we had discussed and prayed for together – literally for years. Why then and not before? I truly don't know.

Metaphorical scales fell from my eyes that evening. That impartation opened my mind, emotions, and will to the other gifts of the Spirit. And, by God's grace, since that tap on my shoulder and the laying on of hands, I've experienced all nine.

Some would argue the speaking in tongues I experienced is not the gift of tongues listed by Paul in 1 Corinthians 12:10. Their interpretation is this gift, in context, is referencing the public use of tongues for the purpose of comforting, edifying, and exhorting one another – especially when followed by the gift of interpretation.

Others point out the plural usage, "different kinds of tongues" as "possibly harmonizing the known spoken languages of Acts 2:4-6 and the unknown transrational utterances in Corinthians, designated particularly for praying and singing in the Spirit, mostly for private worship."[1]

Each would agree that tongues has both a private and public use. For the purposes of this book we will look primarily at the private use of tongues, especially since this use is often linked to the ongoing Spirit in-filling (Ephesians 5:18, 1 Corinthians 14:14-15) which is essential to moving in the nine Gifts.

Definition of the Gift of Tongues

An utterance that is spontaneous, yet inspired by the Holy Spirit, using one's own voice, but where the words and/or syllables are not previously learned by the speaker.

> It's not a seizure of one's will, but a partnership with you and God.

It is a divine collaboration with the Holy Spirit. The speaker opens their mouth to speak and the Spirit fills it with speech that can be either an unlearned actual language (by the speaker) or an utterance that is directly speaking to God – an unlearned prayer language. It's not a seizure of one's will, but a partnership with you and God.

There are three distinct manifestations of tongues in the Bible:

- A language (see Acts 2) where the speaker does not know the language, but when they speak it, it is understood by those whose language it is. It's considered a sign to the unbeliever. (1 Corinthians 14:22; Acts 2:12)

- A language not known by the speaker, not necessarily of human source, possibly angelic (see 1 Corinthians 13:1) done in public worship to edify the body. It should be followed by an interpretation and is divinely inspired by the Holy Spirit. (1 Corinthians 14:27)

- A language, not known by the speaker, usually associated with a private prayer language, not needing interpretation. It's purpose is not communal, but to edify the speaker. (1 Corinthians 14:4-5; Jude 20, 21)

The Bible clearly distinguished between praying in our learned language and praying in an unknown prayer language. 1 Corinthians 14 clarifies:

> ...*I will pray with the spirit, and I will also pray with the understanding...* 1 Corinthians 14:15

According to Dr. Jack Hayford,

"While we may not understand the words we are speaking, spiritual language is not meaningless or gibberish; it is begotten by the Holy Spirit. The Bible says, 'There are... so many kinds of languages in the world and none of them without significance.' (1 Corinthians 14:10)"[2]

> *He who speaks in a tongue does not speak to men but to God, for no one understands him...* 1 Corinthians 14:2

Note the phrase, "for no one understands him." This indicates the difference between a personal prayer language and the public use in Acts 2.

Again, insightfully, Dr. Hayford writes:

"While we don't know what we are saying, we do know to Whom we are speaking, as well as the texture of what our heart feels toward Him, as the Holy Spirit enables us to speak beyond the words we know."[3]

...however, in the Spirit he speaks mysteries.
1 Corinthians 14:2

Paul elaborates what is obviously a "non-conceptual communication directly with God."[4] In the Spirit, we can speak and understand mysteries such as what Paul declares in Colossians 1:27, "This mystery is Christ in you, the hope of glory." Yet, the deep understanding of this scripture can only be revealed by the Spirit communicating with our spirit.

Tongues as Prayer

Tongues, as a prayer language, is primarily given to benefit ourselves.

He who speaks in a tongue edifies himself, but he who prophesies edifies the church. **1 Corinthians 14:4**

It's given to build up our relationship with the Lord, to deepen our love for Him. This is, of course, critical when we are called, as our second greatest priority, to love one another.

In my personal experience, this form of personal prayer opened a door to a deeper consciousness of the things of the Spirit. It also is a form of prayer when words seem to fail. Paul seems to be referring to tongues in Romans 8:26, 27,

> *Likewise the Spirit also helps in our weaknesses. For we do not know what we should pray for as we ought, but the Spirit Himself makes intercession for us with groanings which cannot be uttered. Now He who searches the hearts knows what the mind of the Spirit is, because He makes intercession for the saints according to the will of God.*

This fits with what Paul tells the Corinthians:

> *For if I pray in a tongue my spirit prays but my understanding is unfruitful.* **1 Corinthians 14:14**

I like Sam Storm's insights on this:

"Many say; Paul's response to his mind being 'unfruitful' should be to stop speaking in tongues altogether. Shut it down. Forbid it. But that isn't Paul's conclusion. No sooner does he say that his 'mind is unfruitful' than he makes known his determined resolve: 'I will pray with my spirit, but I will pray with my mind also; I will sing praise with my spirit but I will sing with my mind also.' (1 Corinthians 14:15) We know Paul is referring to praying and singing in tongues because in the next verse he describes giving thanks with one's spirit as intelligible to those who may visit the church meeting."[5]

> As we pray in the Spirit, our faith is built up and we start to believe for things that we couldn't believe for before.

As we pray in the Spirit, our faith is built up and we start to believe for things that we couldn't believe for before. Think about Peter. On the night before the Crucifixion he denied that he even knew Jesus. But on the Day of Pentecost, after speaking in tongues by the power of the Holy Spirit, he stood up before the multitude and preached the first Christian sermon and 3,000 people got saved.

We don't always have the time to pray according to our knowledge. However, if you will make a priority of praying in the Spirit, the Spirit will intercede for you and work all things according to God's will.

My schedule is so hectic that I don't have time to stop and pray as much as I really need to sometimes. However, I have learned to pray in the Spirit whenever I can. When I am walking through an airport, driving in a car, or standing in a line, I can pray in the Holy Spirit and know that those prayers are perfectly aligned with God's will. A few minutes of praying in the Holy Spirit may often be more effective than an hour praying in our own wisdom and understanding or according to our own wants and wishes.

Miracles will just start showing up as you pray in the Spirit. As you pray and obey, you will find yourself right in the middle of what God is doing – sometimes without even knowing it. When you do, the power and authority will flow through your life as you yield to God.

We need more warriors getting their marching orders from God, not from the world.

> *The weapons of our warfare are not carnal...*
> 2 Corinthians 10:4

To move in the Spirit, you need to hear from the Spirit. That can come from prayer, reading the Word, and godly counsel, but also directly from the Spirit via tongues.

Tongues as Warfare

We need warriors who fight in the spirit against "powers and principalities." It's not enough to simply battle on an intellectual, academic, even theological level. Sometimes we must battle in the spirit.

Where prophecy can bring comfort and encouragement publically, tongues privately can bring spiritual strength.

Speaking with literal nation changers like Ted Olbrich, Leslie Keegel, and many others, one common practice emerges – spending hours every week speaking in their prayer language. Each of these leaders depends upon tongues to combat the enemy. They each live in regions of the world where demonic realities are exposed and seemingly more commonplace.

Speaking in tongues is an essential gift of the Spirit when doing battle. I believe that is why Paul wrote:

> *I thank my God I speak in tongues more than you all.*
> 1 Corinthians 14:18

He clarifies the purpose of tongues and differentiates this gift from prophecy when he writes:

For he who speaks in a tongue does not speak to men but to God... 1 Corinthians 14:2

Where prophecy can bring comfort and encouragement publically, tongues privately can bring spiritual strength.

I remember talking to a pastor who was working in an extremely difficult area. He shared how missionaries and pastors would come and go regularly, spiritually beaten. The witchcraft in his area was so strong that the missionaries would last only a few months. Then he made this statement, "Where I live, you have to pray at least one hour a day in the Holy Spirit just to survive."

The writing of this book, more than any other I've done, involved a fierce spiritual battle. It got to the point that I asked for prayer from friends due to a deep sense of unworthiness that crept into my soul. I struggle like everyone else at times, but this emotional swing was excessive and I knew it was a "fiery dart."

Ted Olbrich wrote me in response to my plea with some solid advice:

"I can tell you that you are not imagining this onslaught. It is real and it is vicious. The devil will mess with your health, finances and thoughts. The best way to fight is by praying in the Holy Spirit (tongues) at least one hour per day."

Ted continued with more practical insights:

"I know that sounds impossible. I get up early and spend an hour on my treadmill as I pray. Pray while you are driving. Pray in the natural as well, but remember, if there is a specific demonic assignment against this book, they can understand your natural prayers. You need to do both, but focus on the Spirit in this season."

Thanks, Ted. You're right.

> Paul's purpose was found in serving others, but he knew that an empty glass served no one. Tongues filled his vessel.

But Why Tongues?

I thank God that I speak in tongues more than all of you. 1 Corinthians 14:18

But, because Paul's laser-like focus was the building of the Church, he goes on to state:

Nevertheless, in church I would rather speak five words with my mind in order to instruct others, than ten thousand words in a tongue. 1 Corinthians 14:19

Paul's purpose was found in serving others, but he knew that an empty glass served no one. Tongues filled his vessel.

But why would God have us speak words and/or syllables that give us no cognitive understanding? Again, Sam Storm has a wonderful insight:

"One objection to the gift of tongues... is that nothing is of spiritual value unless it passes through the cerebral cortex of the brain and can be cognitively understood. Any notion that the Holy Spirit might engage with the human spirit directly, by-passing our cognitive thought process, is anathema to most evangelicals. If it is to be spiritually profitable it must be intelligible."[6]

Storm goes on to explain the difference between the need for "intelligibility" for the entire body as opposed to the individual believer, who Paul says can be edified and spiritually enhanced while speaking uninterpreted, private tongues.

Why wouldn't every believer want to engage their spirit in prayer? (1 Corinthians 14:14) You are allowing your spirit to commune directly with the Spirit of God. (1 Corinthians 14:2) How amazing is that?

Randy Clark captures my understanding from the first time I spoke with tongues – there was both a childlikeness to it and a starting point for the other gifts.

"To speak in tongues requires a willingness to become like a child – to look foolish or feel foolish for Christ. Many people find that tongues becomes a doorway to other gifts of the Holy Spirit because it gives us practice in yielding to the Spirit without being completely passive."[7]

Becoming childlike in our faith is one of Jesus' key Kingdom principles. He understood that pride and self-reliance hindered the move of the Spirit in each of us. Isn't it just like God to ask us to step out not only in faith, but also to yield in humility when we ask for the gift of tongues?

Plus, it is also completely congruent with the pattern of the Bible, of God partnering with mankind to see His will established. Like all the other gifts, He doesn't seize our free will but chooses to give us the privilege of being his vessel, albeit a jar of clay.

Speaking of free will, Clark goes on to give an excellent analogy to the control dynamic in relation to speaking in tongues. Tongues, as many non-speakers tend to misinform, is not uncontrollable ecstasy.

"A person who speaks in tongues remains fully in control of themselves and can stop and start at will."[8]

Clark goes on to analogize to driving a car:

"To maneuver the car, you need to both press the gas pedal and turn the steering wheel. To begin praying in tongues, you need to begin making sounds (pressing the gas pedal) but then let the Holy Spirit take over (letting Him turn the steering wheel). As we let Him take over our tongue becomes more fluid."[9]

Interpretation of Tongues

Our focus has been on the self-edifying nature of tongues as a prayer language, but there is also a place for tongues' public use in the local congregation. When that occurs, interpretation of the tongue is always to follow.

> *...to another the interpretation of tongues.*
> 1 Corinthians 12:10

> *If anyone speaks in a tongue, let there be two or at the most three, each in turn, and let one interpret.*
> 1 Corinthians 14:27

> *But if there is no interpreter, let him keep silent in church, and let him speak to himself and to God.*
> 1 Corinthians 14:28

Randy Clark writes:

"Interpretation of tongues is a gift that always operates together with a public message given in tongues. It is a supernatural ability to understand the message and to proclaim it in a language understood by the listeners, so that all can be built up."[10]

Clark believes, as do many other Pentecostal scholars, that the interpretation is not a direct word for word translation.

The one who gives the word in tongues may also interpret. Much like prophecy, any interpretation of tongues must pass a basic test of authenticity.

- Is it biblically sound? If an interpretation is even remotely contrary to Scripture or is extra-biblical (a new revelation not in the Word) it needs to be corrected publicly.

- Does it build up people? This doesn't mean that a tongue might not bring a warning, but always in love and not with a judgmental spirit.

  "Even a stern word can have a powerfully edifying effect if the speaker is motivated by genuine love for God's people."[11]

- Is it focused on Christ? If a tongue is focused on self or things other than Christ, be wary. All attention must stay on Jesus.

- Is it in order? If the pastor is in the middle of his sermon and someone interrupts to speak in tongues, it's probably out of order.

  But all things (tongues, prophecy) *should be done decently and in order.*
  1 Corinthians 14:39-40

Tongues with interpretation is similar to prophecy because of the desired outcome – edification for the body.

Tongues for the Public

I wish you all spoke with tongues, but even more that you prophesied; for he who prophesies is greater than he who speaks with tongues, <u>unless indeed he interprets, that the church may receive edification.</u> (underlining mine) 1 Corinthians 14:5

Paul is qualifying his statement of prophecy over tongues – when interpretation is involved. Tongues with interpretation is similar to prophecy because of the desired outcome – edification for the body. This is a clear understanding of the public versus private role of tongues within the church and for the individual believer.

Paul goes on in this chapter to emphasize this point again:

Even so you, since you are zealous for spiritual gifts, let it be for the edification of the church that you seek to excel. Therefore let him who speaks in a tongue pray that he may interpret. 1 Corinthians 14:12-13

But in verse 22 Paul adds another component to the use of tongues in the public gathering. He also indicates the difference and distinction between tongues and prophecy.

Therefore tongues are for a sign, not to those who believe but to unbelievers; but prophesying is not for unbelievers but for those who believe.

What is the "sign" Paul is referring to? Most believe the word for "sign" is the Greek word *semeion* and is used in a negative sense. When used in a public setting, without interpretation, the first century Jewish person would interpret unknowable speech as a sign of judgment from God. That is why Paul quotes Isaiah 28:11 referring to a warning of God to Israel in Deuteronomy 28:49, that God will send an army speaking a foreign language as a sign of judgment against rebellion – a warning they scoffed at and rejected.

But remember this is in reference to public tongues and not private usage that Paul encourages.

In the next verse, Paul implies the need for limited use of tongues and for their interpretation in a public setting, especially when non-believers can wander in.

> *Therefore if the whole church comes together in one place, and all speak with tongues, and there come in those who are uninformed or unbelievers, will they not say that you are out of your mind?* 1 Corinthians 14:23

Paul seems to be indicating a scenario, possibly a problem in the Corinthian church, where they all just spoke in tongues without interpretation, and therefore lacked any edification for the person who came into this meeting without understanding.

The interpretation of tongues, like a prophetic utterance, has a powerful impact on the non-believer.

> *But if all prophesy, and an unbeliever or an uninformed person comes in, he is convinced by all, he is convicted by all.* 1 Corinthians 14:24

How are they convinced and convicted? You've got mail – divine mail.

> *And thus the secrets of his heart are revealed; and so, falling down on his face, he will worship God and report that God is truly among you.* 1 Corinthians 14:25

I'll never forget the story my older sister told me when I was a young boy. She was 18 and I was 10. Neither of us knew the Lord, but we sensed God's presence in our lives. Her story of encountering the supernatural left me with a desire to not only learn about God, but to also experience Him.

At age 18, my sister, Nancy, already married and with a child, worked in a small factory doing repetitive labor. Because our parents had never gone to church, our only "spiritual" experience involved watching movies like *The Robe* or *The Greatest Story Ever Told* during the Easter season. To break up her monotonous routine, two fellow employees gave her an orange booklet to read during breaks – it was the Gospel of John. She devoured it, reading it everyday, not knowing how deeply it was penetrating into her heart.

Broke and with no insurance, Nancy learned she needed surgery to remove a mass on her pancreas, which doctors warned her could burst and kill her at anytime. The little orange book, along with encouragement from the two Christian employees, gave her enough faith to cry out to God, "Please, Heavenly Father, in Jesus' name, heal me!" The day before the scheduled surgery the surgeons could not find the mass. God had completely healed her.

Another employee of the factory, an older, divorced Catholic woman, angry at the Church and at life in general, was encouraged by her daughter to go to a small Pentecostal church in the area. "I'll only go if Nancy goes," she told her daughter, secretly hoping Nancy would decline. But the three women went on a Wednesday night having no idea what they would encounter.

During worship, Nancy felt a hand on her back and heard words from someone, "Time to go forward." She stepped out and the pastor gently put his hand on her forehead. Because Nancy had a shattered tailbone, the idea of falling backward would normally terrify her. However, the power of the Spirit of God pushed her backward. With no one pushing and no one catching, she, in her own words, "floated" down on her back, free of pain and full of peace.

While on the ground, she heard her older friend singing in a strange language. None of the three had ever heard of an encounter of speaking in tongues before. She looked at Nancy with a full smile proclaiming, "I got baptized in the Holy Spirit." According to

I personally contend that the Gifts, when ministered in love, are the most powerful tools of evangelism the Church has today.

Nancy, the woman, from that moment on, became a totally different person – at work she was no longer angry and bitter, but happy and peaceful.

It would be a few years before Nancy and I would give our hearts to Christ and become disciples. Yet, both of us encountered the God of the supernatural, she experiencing it firsthand and me hearing it from someone I completely trusted.

These supernatural moves of God not only set the table for our future salvation, but also planted faith in us to believe in a God who would willingly touch His creation.

Interpreted tongues, prophecy, and healing all can have a powerful impact on non-believers if they are exercised properly and in order for...

> ...*God is not the author of confusion but of peace...*
> **1 Corinthians 14:33**

In fact, I personally contend that the Gifts, when ministered in love, are the most powerful tools of evangelism the Church has today. This is especially true for a young generation, a post-modern generation that is less concerned about doctrine, theology, and apologetics. They want to know if "it's real," meaning, can it be experienced? Of course, it is not an "either/or" proposition, but "both/and."

Let all things be done decently and in order.

1 Corinthians 14:40

How to Position Yourself for this Gift

As Paul mentions the different kinds of tongues, receiving this gift (or gifts) can differ. There are basic "positionings" mentioned in other chapters that can prepare your heart, mind, soul, and spirit to receive from the Lord.

If the specific tongues gift is an actual language unknown to you but known to your listeners, it normally occurs at the moment needed. It will come and go for a specific purpose – communicating the gospel message. You should be open for the possibility should you be in a place where speaking in a language will maximize the acceptance of the message. Again, as mentioned before, your will is not subjugated; you must open your mouth if prompted by the Spirit.

I remember a story of an American soldier serving in Japan who married a Japanese woman. After moving to the U.S. they started going to church. She attended to honor him but had not accepted Jesus as her savior.

One day he responded to an altar call and she felt the need to support him by also going forward. While waiting to be prayed for, this woman overheard a man speaking and worshiping in tongues. This was all very new to her until his words turned into fluent, perfect Japanese, "You have tried Buddha, and you have tried Zen, why not try me? My name is Jesus Christ."

Needless to say, salvation came to their household on that glorious day.

There are so many wonderful stories, especially from missionaries, where they or someone they were ministering to spoke in the native language – bringing glory to God.

With the growing opportunities and challenges to reaching unreached people groups living in our neighborhoods, should we not be asking the Lord to give us "tongues" to share the gospel? I'm not suggesting we forgo the hard work of building relationships or learning a new language; I'm only wondering if speaking a few fluent sentences about Jesus via the Holy Spirit might break through the difficult cultural barriers.

In these last days, things of the Spirit will be accelerated. We must be open to new ways and methods from the Lord. Nothing blesses people from other nations more than when you attempt to speak their language – can you imagine speaking it, perfectly, through the Holy Spirit?

Positioning Yourself for Your Prayer Language

As I wrote in the beginning of this chapter, my prayer language did not come easily for me. For many, if not most who have asked for this gift, their journey, thankfully, lacked my drama.

So, what are some practical things to consider when asking the Lord for your prayer language?

1. Know the Word of God encourages you to speak in tongues.

2. Know that despite what the world says, the Word says it is a natural part of the Christian experience.

3. Know that you can pray with your mind, but God gives us the additional option to pray with our spirit also.

4. Ask someone with this gift to lay hands on you to receive it.

5. You may want to begin by praising God with your own language, open to the Lord filling your mouth with His language.

Remember, if your earthly father will give you good gifts, how much more your Heavenly Father will give good gifts – "to those who ask Him." (Matthew 7:11)

Never be afraid to ask!

I've seen many people receive this gift spontaneously without any instruction or encouragement, but sometimes believers need some level of instruction and/or assistance. Dr. Steve Schell lists seven very practical suggestions in helping others receive the gift of tongues.[12]

1. Assess where the person is spiritually: Are they saved, and if so, for how long? Have they already had a powerful encounter with God? Were they permanently changed by that encounter? What have they been taught about speaking in tongues, if anything? Do they understand the purpose of tongues? Is the power of the Holy Spirit present at that moment? If not, it would be best to worship and praise freely until the atmosphere changes. Is there any physical evidence that the Spirit has already begun to move upon this person (weeping, trembling, weakness, excitement, joy, a consciousness of God's presence, unusual freedom in worship or prayer, spontaneous confession of sin, etc.)? Does he or she need to be baptized with the Holy Spirit or has that event already happened, and what they need from you is merely help to receive tongues?

2. Explain that speaking in tongues is inspired speech, not compulsive speech. Tell them that they must actively engage their tongue, lips, breath, etc. If they will begin making sounds, the Spirit will form those sounds into words to

speak. Those words seem to rise up from the "belly"; they are not invented in the mind.

3. Explain: "Here's what we're going to do."

- We'll pray, specifically thanking God for giving you this gift when you received Jesus as your Lord and Savior, and then we will ask Him to help you receive what already belongs to you.

- Lay your hand (or hands) on their forehead or the back of their head. Ask permission before you do this, and if they prefer that you not, remember that it is not necessary to lay on hands since Jesus is the Baptizer with the Holy Spirit. It is often helpful to do so, but it is not essential.

- Tell them, "I'm going to begin speaking in tongues loud enough to give you some privacy, and then I would like you to place your thoughts on Jesus and speak to Him, not in our own language but with those words that will well up from within you."

- Explain that they need to be willing to make sounds that aren't words they recognize. At some point, if they will take that step, they'll sense a flow of words being given to them by the Holy Spirit.

- Do not ask them to mimic what you are saying. Do not suggest that they repeat a nonsense phrase to get them started. Assure them that God will provide them with their own language(s). If we manipulate a person into saying something that is self-generated they will lose the joy of their encounter and later question the reality of this gift.

4. Listen to their progress:

    - If tongues have begun, encourage the person to enunciate those words and speak them out boldly.

    - If the person is not able to speak, listen for the Spirit's instructions. He may give you a "word of knowledge" or some other prophetic insight to reveal what is obstructing the person's progress.

    - If they have remained silent, encourage them to step out and try, but assure them that you are not evaluating them and there is no need to perform for you. You are only there to help.

    - Ask, "What's happening? Do you sense that God is doing something?"

- If you believe the Lord has shown you an obstacle, share it humbly and then ask them if what you've said is helpful. If not, move on.

- Ask, "Would you like to continue trying?" If not, remind them that God can meet them when they are alone just as well.

- Assure them that their inability to speak yet does not indicate that they are not fit to receive. God is not withholding this gift, they are simply learning how to receive it.

- Pray for the Lord to continue the work He has begun in them.

- Assure them that you, or someone else, will be available again, if needed, and that you are prepared to walk with them through this process until they finally receive the gift of tongues.

5. Encourage the person who has begun speaking in tongues to continue speaking for a while. Let them freely pour out their heart to God. There is often some form of inner healing going on. Be sensitive not to intrude if they are having a deep encounter, but when the time seems right, ask them to switch back to their own language and praise God with the understanding. Then, after a brief season of free praise, ask

them to return to tongues, so they learn by experience that they can access this gift whenever they wish. Move from one to the other several times.

6. Encourage the person to speak in tongues and even sing in tongues (1 Corinthians 14:15) when they have a private moment later that day, and continue doing so each day until it becomes a beautiful part of their pattern of worship and prayer.

7. Thank God together for His faithfulness.

Chapter Fourteen

The Parable of the Talents and the Flasher

So what does the new Kingdom warrior look like? Someone like Gia – a sexual abuse survivor who, though still dealing with the scars of the past, moves powerfully in the gifts of the Spirit. Or Mike, a veteran of war, physically disabled and limited by constant pain to deep times of intercession, yet still doing Kingdom work. Maybe El Sim, a warrior, all 4' 6" of her, baptizing thousands, seeing miracles, caring for the poor, even as she was poor.

The answer lies within all of their stories. The person God will use will be the person who will let God use them. And they freely offer to serve Him with all they have. There are no disqualifying characteristics. Nothing in one's past can limit the present. No pain, emotional or physical, will stop them.

There are no restrictions due to age, gender, race, or status – those are created by humans, but we serve the Creator.

The generation that will usher in the Kingdom, possibly even the Coming King, will not depend on the skills the world gives, but on the talents that come from above. The following parable, told by Jesus in the context of His second coming, is for the purpose of teaching us how to prepare for His return.

The Parable for Our Times

> *For the kingdom of heaven is like a man traveling to a far country, who called his own servants and delivered his goods to them.* Matthew 25:14

Whose goods? His goods. The Master's goods, and He is willing to give them to all His servants.

> *And to one he gave five talents, to another two, and to another one, to each according to his own ability; and immediately he went on a journey.* Matthew 25:15

The Master trusts us with his goods, or gifts. Some are entrusted with more than others, but each one of us is given what we are able to receive. Everyone gets something from the Master. And more can be added if we are faithful.

> *Then he who had received the five talents went and traded with them, and made another five talents. And likewise he who had received two gained two more also.*
> Matthew 25:16-17

The Master's point is clear: The good servant is the servant who uses the goods, the gifts, the Master has given you.

We are not to compare or complain, only to be faithful to what the Lord has given us.

The principle could not be more dramatic: Don't bury the gift God has given you.

But he who had received one went and dug in the ground, and hid his lord's money. Matthew 25:18

The principle could not be more dramatic: Don't bury the gift God has given you. As we'll read further on in this parable, there was a reason this servant failed his Master. It is a reason that plagues the Church to this day and is causing us to lose ground in the Kingdom battle.

After a long time the lord of those servants came and settled accounts with them. Matthew 25:19

This is an obvious reference to the Second Coming. We all must do the work of the Kingdom before He comes. Our Christian culture, currently, has put a large emphasis on *being* over *doing*. There is much benefit to this. Being in the presence of Jesus, developing our inner, spiritual life is critical, but never in lieu of, or replacing, the doing of the Kingdom. One feeds into the other – repeat again and again. You cannot develop your inner life without the test of relationship and serving. You cannot sustain the "outer" life without replenishing the soul and spirit.

> *So he who had received five talents came and brought five other talents, saying, "Lord, you delivered to me five talents; look, I have gained five more talents besides them." His lord said to him, "Well done, good and faithful servant; you were faithful over a few things, I will make you ruler over many things. Enter into the joy of your lord."* Matthew 25:20-21

Verses 22 and 23 say essentially the same thing to the person who received the two talents. The Master is pleased with both.

In the world, both inside and outside the church, faithfulness seems to have lost some of its currency. We tend to judge by looks, charisma, talent, and skills. Yet, faithfulness is the key character trait valued by this master.

Whether you have five talents or two talents is not the issue. The issue is what you do with them. And what is the ultimate result in using them wisely? Pleasing God.

Yes, we can please God. First, by opening the free gift of grace, then by walking in that grace. During our walk, our journey, we will have the opportunity to be faithful to Him. The result for us personally will be a deep inner joy. This is a joy that only walking with God can bring. It is a taste of what we lost when we were expelled from the "cool of the garden."

> *Then he who had received the one talent came and said, "Lord, I knew you to be a hard man, reaping where you have not sown, and gathering where you have not scattered seed. And I was afraid, and went and hid your talent in the ground. Look, there you have what is yours."* Matthew 25:24-25

The third servant hides the Master's talent. Why? The parable gives us some enlightening detail. This servant had a fearful perception of his master as cruel and unfair. His unreasonable fear caused him to make an unwise choice – a choice that would have epic consequences.

Our view of God, our perception both intellectually and emotionally, impacts how we both understand and respond to Him. Because Christianity involves more than a cerebral ascension to a

The Lord is looking for servants that get this – servants that work hard, work smart, and don't make excuses.

set of doctrinal beliefs, our deepest emotional, psychological issues play into how we live out that which we think we know. Some of these challenges are basic. Did you grow up without a father or was he harsh? How does that impact your view of Father God? This is one of the main reasons our response to God must be based on the Scriptures, not our emotions. Of course, this is easier said than done.

Do we see God as unfair? Is He, in your world, cruel and unfeeling? If so, our response will probably be to hide from Him and, of course, hide the gifts He wishes to give us.

> *But his lord answered and said to him, "You wicked and lazy servant, you knew that I reap where I have not sown, and gather where I have not scattered seed. So you ought to have deposited my money with the bankers, and at my coming I would have received back my own with interest."* Matthew 25:26-27

The Master's retort seems to indicate a blunt, "Stop making excuses! I'm the master, you're not." The other two servants understood they were investing his talents and that he would be reaping something they had sown. They knew this was their job and they executed it well. The third servant, misunderstanding the nature and character of his master, plus being lazy, takes the path of least effort and then makes excuses when his master returns.

The Lord is looking for servants that get this – servants that work hard, work smart, and don't make excuses.

Jesus used a similar metaphor when speaking to His disciples after the encounter with the woman at the well. He speaks of fields "white for harvest." His focus is seeing His servants bring in the lost.

And he who reaps receives wages, and gathers fruit for eternal life, that both he who sows and he who reaps may rejoice together. For in this the saying is true: "One sows and another reaps." I sent you to reap that for which you have not labored; others have labored, and you have entered into their labors. **John 4:36-38**

We are entrusted with "talents" from God to see them benefit the King and His Kingdom. They are not primarily for us, but for others. Selfish, fearful, and lazy – not good ingredients to make up the Kingdom warrior.

How you invest in the Kingdom of God on this earth is a huge priority in God's eyes.

So take the talent from him, and give it to him who has ten talents.

For to everyone who has, more will be given, and he will have abundance; but from him who does not have, even what he has will be taken away. And cast the unprofitable servant into the outer darkness. There will be weeping and gnashing of teeth. Matthew 25:28-30

However one interprets the final four statements of this parable, one thing is most definitely true: Being a steward of what the Lord has given you is serious business. How you invest in the Kingdom of God on this earth is a huge priority in God's eyes.

If you are "burying" what God has entrusted you with... beware. I know we live in an age where guilt and remorse are frowned upon. But preparing for His return by doing the work, His work of establishing the Kingdom before His coming, is HIGH on the God priority list. It's time to take inventory and reexamine our lives and our priorities. How do you think the original hearers of Jesus' words felt? At a minimum – convicted!

7 More Lessons from the Parable

Though the talent referenced in the parable was money, it can easily refer to both the natural giftings the Lord has blessed us with, and also the supernatural gifts He desires we move in.

1. We should live life now with an eye toward His coming again. If we do that it changes everything – how we spend money, how we spend time. Our values and priorities adjust accordingly. I agree with the great George Muller:

"When the day of recompense comes our only regret will be that we have done so little for him, not that we have done too much."[1]

I believe the Kingdom warrior will find freedom and confidence living now, because they so look forward to the future return of Christ. They will want to be "armed and ready" with all the gifts He gives.

2. Who will be the people who benefited or who missed out because you hid your talent? What about the word of knowledge that was never spoken that would have unlocked the heart full of shame? Or the gift of healing that never occurred, keeping someone not only continuing with pain but in not seeing the tender mercy of God?

3. If you are faithful, He desires to give you more – certainly not less. Desire to ask for all the Gifts knowing He desires to give them.

4. His "goods" are given to you not because of how smart you are or how beautiful you are, but because the Master wants to trust you with His treasure.

5. Using His gifts means taking risks, not hiding your gift in fear.

6. How you view the Father will impact how you invest in His Kingdom.

7. Let's focus and be faithful on what the Father has given to us, not what He decides to give to others. Don't compare. Bob Goff insightfully states:

"God never compares what he creates."[2]

Take the Bait

I consider myself a pretty good fisherman. So when I saw the boat, rather yacht, we were about to board, I was skeptical. A spectacular specimen, it would be the fine home to twelve Christian leaders, handpicked to fish for some of the less fortunate living in Alaska.

In fairness, the beauty of this "boat" was matched by the quality and quantity of the fishing equipment – many thousands of dollars devoted and invested in fishing. So all twelve of us, excited to fish, watched as the captain took us to the spot, cut the engine, and proclaimed, "Okay, everyone grab a pole, get your hooks out, and get ready to cast out." No greater words for any fisherman.

So I put my hook on and prepared to fish when the captain looks at me and says, "What are you doing?"

I just love feeling stupid so I put up a slight protest, "Well, I'm fishing. I thought you told me that we're gonna catch fish."

He probably sensed my honest bewilderment and softened his bluntness, slightly, "You can't catch fish like that."

"Well, I always thought a hook plus bait equals fish. Right?" My logical equation would surely win the day.

"No, no, no, no. You can't do that yet." Obviously, the captain knew better and proceeded to inform me of Alaskan fishing realities. "The first thing you need to do is put on one of these things. In America it's called a flasher."

I appreciated his clarifying my national status. A flasher, or a lure, consisted of a long, very shiny piece of plastic. It didn't look very appetizing to the fish below, but as the captain explained, "If you don't put this on, the fish will never see your hook and bait." He repeated himself, but I got it the first time.

Then it hit me. And I knew it was the Holy Spirit.

Sometimes we don't catch fish because we don't have the proper lure.

How many know that some of the "fish" out there live in deep darkness? They have their own plans, purposes, and agendas – you better be prepared to attract them.

The Holy Spirit reminded me, Jesus always had a flasher. Jesus had many lures to catch the "fish." The story, appropriately, of the 5,000 and the 4,000 being fed. It got people's attention. Blind seeing, lame walking, lepers clean – flashers! What about the first miracle? Water to wine... Flash! Could you imagine what news spread throughout Galilee? No doubt people talked for some time, "Hey, some guy turned water into wine. Can you believe it?"

And where did Jesus do most of His fishing? In the synagogue? No, out there in the streets, on the hillsides, where the desperate lived.

Wherever He went, He healed, He touched, and even the most darkened heart was opened and amazed. They saw the lure and Jesus hooked them with the Word of God and pulled them into the Kingdom.

> The use of the Gifts, alongside the commands from the Bible to show mercy and to care for the poor, widow, and orphan, is a powerful force.

Lessons from the Boat and the Parable

Throughout the book there's been a description of the believer who moves in the gifts of the Spirit for the purposes of establishing the Kingdom on earth. The approach has been intentionally holistic because Kingdom work is holistic. When we see "the lost" we know that to reach them we must address issues concerning not only their souls but also their situations. The use of the Gifts, alongside the commands from the Bible to show mercy and to care for the poor, widow, and orphan, is a powerful force (Romans 12:4-8).

In fact, the "lures" we as a Church can use to reach the poor among us, like creating micro businesses or building affordable housing, impact not only those in need but also those who look at the Church skeptically. They increasingly see the Church as irrelevant, but are forced to take a second look when the Church cares for the community outside its own walls.

Our church used a massive food and clothing distribution that not only blessed thousands, but also testified to our city. In Papua New Guinea, I saw local churches dig wells, open hospitals and schools – this happens around the globe to tell people in their community that Jesus cares.

Of course "the Church" is you and me. We miss the point if we wait on church leadership to create programs when we are called to carry the challenge. How many church leaders would be thrilled by a congregation of warriors motivated by love, full of the Spirit, and led to establish the Kingdom wherever they go?

My denomination has been led for nearly a decade by a leader who models this lifestyle of charismatic, compassionate activism. Wherever Dr. Glenn Burris Jr. goes, and he has traveled the world many times over, he has demonstrated the power of simple love. He constantly looks to help out the person he encounters in the everyday of life. It might be the person he sits next to on a jet who needs prayer, or the family of five in the restaurant who could use someone to pick up their bill. And he's always listening to the Spirit, asking what He wants to do. I've traveled with him. I know.

More Flashers

Just when I thought my pole was ready to cast, the captain returned, "Stop! It's not ready yet!"

"Why?" I feebly replied.

"Because you're throwing it out onto the top; the fish aren't there. The fish are down deeper. You've gotta get your flasher, hook, and bait down deeper."

I will show you where you need to go to reach the harvest; but you must listen to Me – not your agenda, your plans. I will show you where to catch people.

The captain proceeded to show me a large monitor screen that indicated the depth of the fish – 60 feet, 90 feet, 120 feet. And then the Holy Spirit spoke to me again.

"That monitor is like Me, the Holy Spirit, and I will show you where the fish are. I will show you where to put your hook and bait. I will show you where you need to go to reach the harvest; but you must listen to Me – not your agenda, your plans. I will show you where to catch people."

We need to be hooked up to the power. The fastest growing churches today are those that are open and moving in the power of the Holy Spirit. *And you will receive power.* (Acts 1:8) To feel good? To be blessed? No, to reach the fish.

My next question to the Captain, now that I was thoroughly humbled and teachable, "Okay, I see that. But how do I get my hook down there?"

He showed me a big ball of lead with a measurement wheel, "And together, they will take you to the depth that the monitor says the fish are. You lock it in and that's where you drag your flasher, bait, and hook."

We must focus where the "fish" are and drag our "flasher" under the wisdom of the Holy Spirit.

One of the greatest ministries in Los Angeles is Angelus Temple and the Dream Center. They reach into the darkest corners, but always under the leading of the Holy Spirit. Its pastor and leader, Matthew Barnett, really started the ministry when the Lord told him to take his desk and office out on the street – where the hurting people are!

What did the religious people get so upset with Jesus about? "That Jesus... He's always with those sinners!"

There is a harvest. Are we only fishing on top of the water – catching the same fish and throwing them back for some other fisherman to hook – instead of going deeper for fish that have never seen the light?

Then the Lord taught me my final lesson from this Alaskan experience.

Along with the others, I caught the first fish and it would be the biggest fish – a King Salmon. I ended up catching the most fish on the trip that was cold and rainy.

Remember, this was a yacht with staterooms and snack bars – everything beautiful and heated down below. The other 11 stayed below but I kept fishing. Why? Because that was our assignment. I fished four poles at once, looking at the monitor, lowering down the line, changing bait – catching fish. Lots of fish.

Out on the deck, cold and raining very hard, I hooked a big one. So I screamed up to the captain, "Fish on!" And he stopped the boat so that I could reel in my fish.

Someone came out from the nice, warm lounge and slapped me on the shoulder, "You've got the fishing anointing."

I smiled back, but it hit me hard. There was no fishing anointing. I caught fish because I stuck with it. I caught fish because I learned the lessons from the captain. I caught fish because I ignored the cold and the rain.

As I walked out of the cold into the warmth of the luxury cabin, it was as if everything turned to slow motion. I looked at the other 11. One sat in his chair praying. A few were reading their Christian books and Bibles. The rest of the fishermen were fellowshipping, all with coffee and tea and cakes, having a wonderful time.

I know when the Holy Spirit speaks. And He spoke loud and clear. This wasn't me feeling sorry for myself or being self-righteous. The only reason I tell the story is because of what the Holy Spirit said in that very moment – because it's so critical.

"That's my Church. But they have forgotten their assignment. They are enjoying the fellowship. They are enjoying my Word. They are enjoying my blessing. But they forgot their assignment – go into the world and preach the gospel."

Jesus' first words, "I'll make you fishers of men." His last word, "Go." He also adds at the end the issue of authority, power. "All authority has been given to me in heaven and on earth."

On earth as it is in heaven. Jesus has given us authority:

And these signs will follow those who believe.

Mark 16:17

Chapter Fifteen

Full Throttle in the Church

"Because the Holy Spirit of God is a promise to be received, then He is a power to be released (and a person to be recognized). So why are we so pathetic? Why are there so many in the church, yet we are doing so little?"[1]

- Kenneth C. Ulmer, James O. Davis

In fairness to global leaders Bishop Ulmer and Dr. Davis, they answer their stinging questions in their excellent book *The Forgotten Baptism*.

"The presence and power of the Holy Spirit is not an additional, optional extra, but the very essence of a life lived in relationship to Jesus, who was anointed by the same Holy Spirit that would resurrect Him..."

They go on to ask another question, one that every church must embrace, "If the Son of the living God lived in the anointing of the Holy Spirit, how much more do we likewise need that same power! God the Father so loved us that He makes available to us the very same Holy Spirit power that raised Jesus the Son from the grave."[2]

The 5 Essentials

Moving in the gifts of the Spirit involves the context of the local church. The manifestation of the Gifts may take place in the marketplace or private setting, but always are inspired, demonstrated, and taught in a body of believers.

As mentioned before, the natural flow of these Gifts is an essential part of the Kingdom dynamic since Pentecost and the first church. Those leaders and churches wishing to continue in this Kingdom quest must be willing to step out not only in teaching, but also in practice of God's presence. Of course, this assumes biblical orthodoxy and orthopraxy.

Here are five essential qualities of the church and church leaders committed to bringing the Kingdom "on earth as it is in heaven."

- Churches that will usher in the Kingdom will be led by servant leaders who have experienced not only the power of His resurrection, but also the fellowship of His sufferings.

- Churches that will usher in the Kingdom will be led by prophetic leaders who will empower and commission the next generation to reach the lost utilizing the gifts of the Spirit.

- Churches that will usher in the Kingdom will be led by diverse leaders who represent and understand the needs of their community and of the world and meet them by the gifts and fruit of the Spirit.

- Churches that will usher in the Kingdom will be led by bold leaders who fear God and not man, and will teach and lead by biblical, not cultural, values.

- Churches that will usher in the Kingdom will be led by hungry leaders who desire the presence of God more than the praise of the world.

This list isn't in priority nor exhaustive. As you read on please consider where you may fit in now or grow into for the future. A church is only as effective as its people.

Yet, if we are honest, our preference is for His power rather than His sufferings.

I will build my church and the gates of hell will not prevail against it. Matthew 16:18

Essential #1 The Church of Power and Suffering

That I might know Him and the power of His resurrection, and the fellowship of his sufferings, being conformed to His death. Philippians 3:10

How much do we really want to know Him? The Apostle Paul's question must be answered if we desire to move in His gifts. Yet, if we are honest, our preference is for His power rather than His sufferings. Yet, both come in the package marked "discipleship."

Kingdom leaders, Kingdom people will experience both power of His resurrection and pain of His suffering. It is the divine balance necessary to be conformed to the Incarnated One – to represent Him to a world hungry for real Christians.

Former missionary and now lead pastor of Westside Church in Bend, Oregon, Steve Mickel, understands this all too well. In his excellent book, *Walking in the Dark*, Steve, a personal friend, tells of his and his wife's, Suzanne's, journey after the tragic death of Chase, the eldest of their four sons.

"After Chase died, I wondered about God being in control... suffering in the world causes us to question the very existence of God, not to mention His ability to stop tragedy."[3]

Steve and Suzanne's sojourn took them beyond trite answers and flippant replies to the problem of pain. Steve, in his own words, was "furious" with God. There were no neat answers or tidy conclusions, only questions. But the trial ultimately proved to deepen their faith.

"I can't tell you exactly when things changed between me and God... but there was a moment when I realized God wasn't responsible for my son's death, even though He is sovereign. I didn't come to this conclusion because of what I know about God from the Bible, or even past experiences, or what others had told me about Him. I knew it because I finally let go of my defenses and my efforts to understand, and I stood there in His embrace as we both wept over the death of my child. I didn't stop asking questions; I never will. But I no longer let the questions keep me from intimacy with God."[4]

Their lives and the ministry of their church reflect the balance between resurrection power and fellowshipping with the suffering.

Steve's honesty is a beacon, especially to a younger generation who seeks faith forged not in rules, but deep relationship.

"So, I am trying to live like Chase, to be all in with God's love. No holding back, no hedging my bets. But the only way I can live this way is by keeping my eyes on Jesus."[5]

Resurrection Power

In the affluent suburb of Lake Forest, California, Dr. Clayton Robinson leads his congregation with a teaching rich in the Word of God, complemented from his vast theological pedigree. The members of the Connection Church know that biblical scholarship and the moving of the Holy Spirit are not mutually exclusive. This was never more evident than a story shared by Dr. Robinson at a recent denominational convention. There he recounted how one of his staff families prayed for their baby in womb – a baby doctors urged to abort due to severe growth abnormalities. "Being that they were Foursquare ministers, they decided to trust God instead," Clayton shared with the large audience.

At eight months, doctors induced labor on the baby so severely stressed that they warned that this little girl would not survive. But the whole church prayed. Little Brielle came into

Lord, do it again, grow out longer!

the world alive, but facing many medical challenges. At seven months old she was so small and her arms were so tiny that she still wore newborn clothing, her hands barely emerging out of the sleeves. Before a doctor appointment to determine a proper course for treatment, and while father, Michael, was leading worship at the church, mother, Kathleen, holding her baby experienced the gift of faith.

"God, you can heal my baby." Her spoken words released even more faith.

"Arms, grow out in the name of Jesus!"

Suddenly, the baby's tiny hands popped out of the sleeves, perceptible growth, but more needed.

"Lord, do it again, grow out longer!"

Kathleen looked at the length of her baby's arms and declared a third time, "Lord, do it again." This time, Brielle's arms grew to normal length making her outfit look "rather silly."

Arms which barely reached her belly, now reached fully to her knees. The doctors declared her perfectly normal and no more medical follow-up necessary.

Dr. Clayton was quick to point out that this healing did not occur during a church healing service, but through the faith of a mother. Yet, that personal faith grew in a congregation that boldly teaches, "Jesus Christ is the same yesterday, today, and forever." (Hebrews 13:8)

The Church must welcome both the fellowship of sufferings and the power of His resurrection through their doors. The world will take notice; it always does when the Kingdom of God comes.

Do you believe these children can use My gifts?

Essential #2 The Church of the NextGen

Can children move in the gifts of the Spirit? The answer, according to the many children's pastors I've spoken to is, "Why not?"

NextGen Leader and Children's Gospel Box Director Rev. Natalie Werking states humorously and insightfully, "They (the children) receive the same Holy Spirit (adults do), not the junior size version," and goes on to add, "because of their childlike faith they have less trouble operating in the Gifts."

In fact, kids often lack the inhibitions usually reserved for teens and adults. However, it becomes the role of the Church to provide an environment that allows children a safe place to move in the Spirit.

Rev. Brooke Bourg, NextGen pastor of Vision Church, Louisiana does just that. The Lord challenged her early in her ministry:

"Do you believe these children can use My gifts?"

Nearly every service allows for the Gifts to be manifested with kids giving prophetic words, laying on of hands, tongues and interpretation of tongues. After all, Pastor Brooke believes they are "not too young to hear from God." Of course, this happens with frequency because she and her leaders both encourage and expect it. That translates to the kids, who often express prophetic words in the main adult services as well.

"Don't shy-out, be bold. Let God use you!" Brooke is fond to challenge her kids and teens alike.

A good word for adults, too.

So, can children take the Gifts into the marketplace? Can they win the lost? Touch the suffering? Once again, the answer must be, "Why not?"

Ted and Sou Olbrich's amazing ministry in planting churches and orphanages in Cambodia is due in large part to their mobilization of the NextGen. They fully expect their young people, from ages 10 to young adult, to move in all the gifts of the Spirit – even outside the safe confines of the church.

Most of their youth have been raised in their orphan homes, nourished in the Word of God, expecting the supernatural. The first group to form a team that went out to win the lost through signs and wonders, village-by-village, called themselves the Young Tigers. They were made up of young pastors and young adults. This group inspired a younger group of high school age teens to do the same. They nicknamed themselves the Young Lions. Junior High age groups followed, moving in power evangelism as effective as the others. Together, these young people brought a fierce faith combined with an innocence to take on the very real spiritual darkness facing all believers.

According to the ministry, "Much of our growth is through the Young Tigers, Lions, and Fishermen – Spirit-filled youth teams that are seeing the book of Acts come alive in Cambodia. They go out in one weekend and leave behind hundreds of new Christians."

On one such weekend these teams converged on a piece of prime real estate needed to build another orphanage. Its extremely low price caused suspicions that were confirmed when the youth teams arrived. This land was once part of the infamous "Killing Fields" used to slaughter hundreds of thousands of Cambodians during the regime of the dictator Pol Pot.

Terrified local neighbors avoided the area, seeing "ghosts." A small cottage industry of tourists emerged wanting to experience this "haunted" ground. Fear dominated the area until the youth teams came armed in prayer, bold faith, and a purity of innocence to break any and all demonic strongholds. The sightings ended, the fear subsided, an orphanage was built. And, a neighborhood witnessed a power encounter where the Kingdom of God wins because young people were trusted to lead the way.

What's Your Name?

One of my favorite stories of all time involves an obscene word. Yes, you read that correctly. I would never use such a word, even in a shortened, less offensive form, if it wasn't so essential to the story – a powerful encounter with the Gifts and a child's purity.

It came to me from a trusted friend and fellow Youth With A Mission (YWAM) missionary.

A team comprised mainly of the children of YWAM parents toured Europe doing what YWAM does effectively: sing, skits, and share. The typical outreach involved a skit or singing with each child asking the Lord who in the crowd they should witness to.

On this particular day in some country in Europe, an 8-year-old boy, the son of this group's leader, asked the Lord who he should speak with. Billy knew how to hear His Father's voice and also to respect his earthly father's rules. So, he approached his dad after their music set and pointed to the man he wanted to speak with.

His father was afraid. The large man identified by his son not only looked angry, he wore provocative women's clothes.

"Are you sure, Billy? Are you sure that is the person the Lord wants you to speak to?"

"Yes, Daddy. Jesus wants me to talk to him," his son answered back, full of unquestioned faith.

So father and son approached the man in the woman's clothing. Father prayed silently a short distance away while Billy put out his hand asking the man, "What's your name, mister?"

Now even angrier, the man looked down to the boy, trying to scare him away. "F-off, kid!" he used the full, obscene word.

In that very moment the power of innocence, the burden of sin, and the presence of the Holy Spirit intersected. Little Billy smiled while answering back, "Hello Mr. F-off! My name is Billy. Nice to meet you."

I'm not sure about the details of the rest of the story. All I was told is that the man in the woman's clothing began to sob, uncontrollably. The innocence of this obedient boy, obviously not knowing the profane nature of the word he spoke, struck directly into the man's heart. Stone cracked exposing flesh. Old became new.

The man gave his life that day to the very Jesus Billy brought with an innocent introduction. He stayed with the team as they continued their tour.

Could it be that children, unafraid, faith-filled, full of the Holy Spirit might be the priority of the Lord in seeing His Kingdom established?

And could it be that like the disciples, the Church today might be guilty of discouraging the little ones from the presence of Jesus? Maybe not in an obvious manner, but in ignorance and indifference, nonetheless.

Let's encourage our kids to be in His presence, hear His voice, trust them to go, and then get out of the way.

Essential #3 The Church of the Diverse Reaching the Diverse

Surekha and Chrishani Hulugalle, Sri Lankans by birth, serve as national leaders in one of the darkest regions on earth. Not the jungles of Central Africa, or the sands of the Middle East, but on the foggy island of England.

Long considered a post-Christian continent, Western and Eastern Europe's landscape is filled with empty cathedrals and cold hearts, the bitter fruits of humanism and secularization. According to two PhDs on the subject of European evangelism, "Europeans seem to retain an attitude of mistrust towards evangelical religion."[6]

Yet, despite these forces, their churches and others across the continent are beginning to thrive. "Over recent decades Pentecostal, Charismatic growth in Europe has received impetus from transnational movements such as John Wimber's Vineyard, the 'Toronto Blessing,' and Pensacola revival. By far the largest growth of Pentecostalism, however, is due to the presence of migrants from many parts of the globe."[7]

The Hulugalles are a dynamic part of that presence. Mentored in Sri Lanka by Dr. Leslie Keegel, they know first hand the hard fought battles in Kingdom warfare.

Their church, and the churches in their oversight, know that to penetrate the powerful forces of secularism they must demonstrate, as Jesus did, the gospel in its fullness. This specifically means moving in all the gifts of the Holy Spirit. But also, being a church that reflects the changing ethnic makeup of England.

On any typical meeting or outreach conducted in England or other European nations, the Hulugalles and team see God consistently move in power. For example, a woman with a brain tumor the size of a tennis ball was in a coma for three months.

Within 24 hours of praying over her, the tumor vanished and she came out of the coma completely healed.

In another instance, their young group of teens, in school to learn how to move in the Gifts, went out into the streets and found a Hindu man suffering from a stroke, left leg paralyzed. After praying for him, he was totally restored.

Yet another testimony from a "street team" saw one woman walking with an obvious physical disability. Sitting at a bus stop, they asked her politely if they could pray for her. Hearing that she suffered back pain, they laid hands on her. After a few minutes of praying, she began to weep and proclaimed all her pain totally left and she experienced a miracle.

The stories could fill a book. (I'm hoping they will write one!)

According to Surekha, "So often we tend to depend on the 'human factor' that the Holy Spirit takes second place. This is in fact idolatry." The key, according to him and so many

Modern religion focuses upon filling churches with people. The true gospel emphasizes filling people with God.

emerging leaders in Europe, "It is about our hearts hungering after Him… it is about our hearts seeking Him."[8]

The Hulugalles would agree with what A.W. Tozer said years ago, "Modern religion focuses upon filling churches with people. The true gospel emphasizes filling people with God."

All people, every nation.

Essential #4 The Church of the Bold and Biblical

The Holy Spirit fell powerfully on a young man raised in the steamy bogs of the Bayou.

Kim Voisin's career in illegal narcotics started at age 12. His scrappy fearlessness would serve him well. He became a top "bill" collector for the drug cartel. In describing his job description, Kim recalled with the slightest blend of sarcasm and regret:

"I encouraged people to pay."

So when he reluctantly entered the church at the behest of his young wife, Vanessa, he immediately looked for an exit strategy. Sizing up the ushers, Kim took solace in the fact he could "take them." After all, fighting compared favorably to the other joy of his life: hunting alligators.

Fidgeting in the back row, Kim's focus on potential threats kept him oblivious to the moving of the Holy Spirit. Vanessa, knowing how to motivate her husband, nudged him saying, "Look. You're afraid."

Actually, she'd never seen Kim afraid or cry before, but the moment he stepped out from the pew, weeping began. Deep sobs quickly turned into speaking in tongues and an hour later Kim would rise up from the floor and step toward a new life. A completely unique experience would become an essential part of his daily life.

Kim's boldness and fearlessness only grew as he marched uninvited into a meeting of a cartel leader who had put a contract on his life. Drug organizations typically frown on one of their own leaving the group. "Either release me or kill me now, but I'm not coming back." He left alive.

In two months, after his personal Pentecost, Kim became a youth pastor. Of his first 20 youth in his group, 18 were on full-time probation. Kim found his calling and the state of Louisiana lost a serious drug dealer and gained a Spirit-filled pastor.

With Kim as senior pastor, and wife Vanessa as worship pastor, Vision Church has planted 15 churches throughout the region and influences dozens more. They are a balanced combination of God's power, personal holiness, and social activism. Yet, nothing flows from church life from need, but by anointing. "Is God leading this? If so, anointed leaders will follow," is one of Pastor Kim's foundational ministry axioms.

Today, the church is as comfortable feeding 400 families a month as it is hosting the most powerful politicians in the state. They continue to reach into the world of drugs, which have corrupted their region, with a rehab center the state recognizes and depends upon.

They move in all of the gifts of the Spirit. On any Sunday a visitor will experience prophecy, tongues, and interpretation of tongues during worship. Healing and miracles are a regular occurrence. And this is not limited to adults. Youth and children are taught to move in the presence of God. They expect the gifts of the Spirit to flow through them – even outside the church.

Years after Kim stepped out of the pew he remains unafraid – still bold, yet not reliant upon his own toughness, but dependent upon the powerful presence of God. More importantly he is not alone. He continues to raise up an army of bold leaders, men and women, young and old, to hear God's voice and fear not.

Turkey

The Church is growing throughout the Islamic world through signs and wonders, especially in the area of visions and dreams. The Spirit of fear must be replaced by power, love, and a sound mind. (2 Timothy 1:7) Bold leaders are essential. The nation of Turkey, with less than 1% Christian, is no exception. The cultural and spiritual challenges are enormous. I did a recent conference in Istanbul on the gifts of the Holy Spirit, which was eagerly received. Nearly all were touched by the power and presence of the Holy Spirit. One Turkish lady at this conference began speaking in tongues for the first time and was "slain in the Spirit." After the conference, she and her husband traveled 20 hours southeast to support a house church.

Here's the account from our missionary there in Turkey of what happened:

"While they were having the house meeting, the Holy Spirit suddenly filled the room. Without anyone praying for anyone, people started to go down in the Spirit. Then two people started to speak in tongues for the first time."

This missionary, a young fearless man of God, proclaimed, "What God started in Istanbul through the laying on of hands continues to spread to other believers throughout the country. To God be the glory!"

The Kingdom of God is clashing with the kingdom of darkness. The battle is real. God's army is recruiting. Bold, brave men and women, young and old are needed. The timid, less committed need not apply.

Essential #5 The Church of Intimacy

We've all been there. Wanting more. Of course, the question is, more of what?

That's not a tease or a throwaway line; it's the question we must ask seriously and consider deeply.

More of God? But what does that really mean to you? To me?

To former LIFE College (now University) Academic Dean Dr. Tom Wymore it really meant that he wanted more of God to provide supernatural power flowing out of his ministry. God had another plan.

"I was really motivated for supernatural power, but God rerouted me to intimacy," Tom recalled. Throughout his ministry, Tom always possessed a yearning for more. After all, he studied and taught from great authors like A.W. Tozer and Brother Lawrence.

But, taking that 18-inch trip from the head to the heart proved a challenge. Tom's hunger to know God in a deeper, more intimate place reached a spiritual peak at his denomination's annual convention. There he felt strongly that Dr. Leslie Keegel, a church planter from Sri Lanka, should pray for him. Leslie's prayer initiated a 30-day personal revival, culminating in an event that would impact the trajectory of his life and ministry.

In an intense time of prayer on the 30th day, Tom cried out to God, "I'm not leaving until you show up!" Three hours of prayer later the Lord spoke. Tom realized at that moment He had been speaking all along. The Lord instructed him to take the time, the three hours of intimate prayer, as a part of his daily life. Tom protested, "I don't have three hours a day."

He obeyed and after a few months the three hours turned into an ongoing, minute-by-minute, intimate conversation with

God. He had stumbled upon the Apostle Paul's secret, "Pray without ceasing."

Tom wanted more power; God gave him intimacy. Tom desired the Gifts; he got the Giver. Yet, the gifts of the Spirit, flowing through him, radically changed people's lives. Those lives were not limited to inside the sanctuary, but also to the coffee shop, the market, and the park bench. Soon, he coached others to discover and develop their spiritual gifting.

A personal tragedy forced Tom to a deeper place – a space few go and fewer choose. His beloved wife, Jenny, developed pancreatic cancer. Tom and Jenny joined the

> **Life in the Spirit is really just life as it was meant to be – a walk with Father in the cool of the Garden.**

"fellowship of His sufferings" and faced the ultimate test, the crucible of faith. Pain on the level 10 tormented them both until the Lord touched her. They cherished those days before she died in 2010.

Such life experiences are crushing to the soul. The chaff of bitterness and doubt lie waiting on the threshing floor. Tom chose surrender instead. It provided the pathway, a walk with the Spirit he had only read about and hoped for.

Life in the Spirit is really just life as it was meant to be – a walk with Father in the cool of the Garden. Yet, it doesn't shield us from pain, suffering, or sorrow.

People like Tom and Steve Mickel know this all too well. Their lives and moving in the Gifts reflect the Refiner's fire. No charismatic personality can duplicate this. No gifting in the natural will possess its weathered beauty. And most of all, this deeper walk is never satisfied. It always wants more.

"No matter how well we know Him, there's still all of our infinite God left to get to know. So deeper intimacy with Father God is always possible for all of His people, all of the time."[9]

Tom's words are a map on the journey, a north star, positioning us to reach our destination. Yet, we are not arriving to a place, but to a person. We are, like the little children who troubled the disciples, yearning to be in the arms of the Master.

In His embrace all are welcome, no one will be turned away, everyone can play.

Notes

Chapter 1

1. A.J. Swoboda/plenary session 2018 Foursquare Connection, Seattle, May 31

2. Merrill F. Unger, *The Baptism and Gifts of the Holy Spirit*, Chicago, IL, Moody Press, 1974, page 174

3. Facebook post June 30, 2018, Ted Olbrich

4. Twitter@JohnPiper, November 18, 2018, 10:00 am

5. An obvious reference to the teachings of George Eldon Ladd, See *The Gospel of the Kingdom*, Grand Rapids, MI, Paternaster Press, 1959

6. Christine Caine, authenticchristianliving.com

7. Twitter@TullianT, February 19, 2019 4:56 pm

8. Jerry Cook and Stanley C. Baldwin, *Love, Acceptance and Forgiveness: Being Christian in a Non-Christian World*, Minneapolis, MN, Bethany House Publishers, 1979, 2009, page 61

9. A prophetic word delivered by Rev. Clint Pickrel/Foursquare Cabinet, January 2019

Chapter 2

1. Lester Sumerall, *The Gifts and Ministries of the Holy Spirit*, New Kensington, PA, Whitaker House, page 38

2. Christine Caine, christinecaine.com

3. Jerry Cook and Stanley C. Baldwin, *Love, Acceptance and Forgiveness: Being Christian in a Non-Christian World,* Minneapolis, MN, Bethany House Publishers, 1979, 2009, page 65

4. Leslie Keegel, *The Spirit of the Lord is Upon Us,* Anaheim, CA, Foursquare Missions Press, 2017, page 168

5. Bill Johnson, *When Heaven Invades Earth,* Shippensburg, PA, Destiny Image Publishers Inc., 2013 (Expanded Edition), page 262

6. Leslie Keegel, *The Spirit of the Lord is Upon Us,* Anaheim, CA, Foursquare Missions Press, 2017, page 169

7. Leslie Keegel, *The Spirit of the Lord is Upon Us,* Anaheim, CA, Foursquare Missions Press, 2017, page 9

8. Leslie Keegel, *The Spirit of the Lord is Upon Us,* Anaheim, CA, Foursquare Missions Press, 2017, page 9

9. Bill Johnson

10. Christine Caine, christinecaine.com

11. Ed Stetzer, christianitytoday.com, October 12, 2015, *Monday is for Missiology: What is the Missional Church?*

12. Bill Johnson, *Hosting the Presence Unveiling Heaven's Agenda,* Shippensburg, PA, Destiny Image Publishers Inc., 2012, page 30

13. N.T. Wright, *Simply Christian: Why Christianity Makes Sense,* New York, NY, Harper One, 2006, page 100

14. John Wimber/Kevin Springer, *Power Evangelism,* Minneapolis, MN, Chosen, 1986, 2009, page 27

15. Smith Wigglesworth, allchristianquotes.org

16. Dr. Craig Keener, *The Holy Spirit and Reading Scripture*, Article from *Catalyst*, September 5, 2018

17. Daniel Brown, *Enjoying Your Journey with God*, Lake Mary, FL, Charisma House, 2001, page 170

18. Mike Bickle, mikebickle.org, *Growing in the Prophetic*, 2010

19. Glenn Burris, Facebook, May 6, 2018

20. The text in Corinthians refers to the gifts (*charismata*) as spirituals (*pneumatika*) because they are capacities freely bestowed by the Holy Spirit.

21. "Energy" comes from the same root word.

22. This list is limited to 1 Corinthians 12:1-10. Yet, according to the authors of *Foundations of Pentecostal Theology*, "There are many different spiritual gifts, far more than the nine mentioned in 1 Corinthians 12. In fact, there may be as many gifts as there are useful functions in the church or needs in the world." In fact, in 1 Corinthians 12:28 Paul added the gifts of helps and administration. But, for the purposes of this book, we will focus on the nine gifts, breaking them into three categories: The Revelation Gifts – wisdom, knowledge, discerning of spirits; The Power Gifts – faith, healing, miracles; The Inspirational Gifts – prophecy, tongues, interpretation of tongues.

Chapter 3

1. C. Peter Wagner, *Spreading the Fire*, Ventura, CA, Regal Books 1994, page 25

2. C. Peter Wagner, *Spreading the Fire*, Ventura, CA, Regal Books 1994, page 25

3. C. Peter Wagner, *Spreading the Fire*, Ventura, CA, Regal Books 1994, page 25

Chapter 4

1. *The Spirit Filled Bible*, NKJV, Nashville, TN, Thomas Nelson Publishers, 1991, page 1736

2. Christine Caine, christinecaine.com

Chapter 5

1. Christy Wimber, Facebook, October 14, 2018

2. Bill Johnson, *Hosting His Presence* (blog), January 14, 2013

3. R.A. Torrey, www.azquotes.com/quote

4. Andrew Murray, www.beliefnet.com/evangelical

5. G. Campbell Morgan, Grand Rapids, MI, Baker Book House, 1955, page 317

6. A.J. Swoboda/plenary session 2018 Foursquare Connection, Seattle, May 31, 2018

Chapter 6

1. Donald Gee, *Concerning Spiritual Gifts*, Springfield, MO, 2007, (page 438 of 1763 Kindle)

2. Howard Carter, *Questions and Answers on Spiritual Gifts*, Tulsa, OK, Harrison House, Inc., 1976, page 146

3. Howard Carter, *Questions and Answers on Spiritual Gifts*, Tulsa, OK, Harrison House, Inc., 1976, page 146

4. Donald Gee, *Concerning Spiritual Gifts*, Springfield, MO, 2007, (page 414 of 1763 Kindle)

5. David Pytches, *Spiritual Gifts in the Local Church*, Minneapolis, MN, Bethany House Publishers, 1985, page 96

6. David Pytches, *Spiritual Gifts in the Local Church,* Minneapolis, MN, Bethany House Publishers, 1985, page 52

7. Randy Clark and Mary Healy, *The Spiritual Gifts Handbook*, Minneapolis, MN, Chosen Books, 2018, pages 137-138

8. Patrick Mead, Twitter@TravelingMead, November 18, 2018

Chapter 7

1. I recall hearing this story in my MC510 class at Fuller Seminary led by John Wimber and C. Peter Wagner

2. Mike Bickle, *Growing in the Prophetic,* www.mikebickle.org 2010

3. Mike Bickle, *Growing in the Prophetic,* www.mikebickle.org 2010

Chapter 9

1. David Pytches, *Come Holy Spirit*, Minneapolis, MN, Bethany House Publishers, 1985, page 109

2. George Muller, www.goodreads.com

3. Francois Du Toit, twitter@francoislydia, May 22, 2018, 10:17 pm

4. A.W. Tozer, www.revival_library.com

5. Leslie Keegel, *The Spirit of the Lord is Upon Us,* Anaheim, CA, Foursquare Missions Press, 2017, page 170

Chapter 10

1. Regarding the plural use of "gifts of healings," "This suggests there are either many types of healing for

different diseases or that each exercise of healing power is a separate gift." (page 317, Foundations of Pentencostal Theology, Volume 1, Revised and Updated) "The plural suggests that as there are many sicknesses and diseases, the gift is related to healings of many disorders." – *Spirit Filled Bible*, NKJV, Nashville, TN, Thomas Nelson Publishers, 1991, page 1737

2. Bill Johnson, BJM.org/qa@2018

3. David Pytches, *Spiritual Gifts in the Local Church*, Minneapolis, MN, Bethany House Publishers, 1985, page 166

4. Pamela Moore, *The Five Silent Years of Corrie Ten Boom*, Zondervan, 1986, page 189

5. Dr. Todd Hunter is the founding pastor of Holy Trinity Anglican Church in Costa Mesa, California. Facebook, June 15, 2019; 1:06 pm

6. Sally McClung, Facebook, *Prayers for Floyd and Sally McClung*, November 30, 2018

7. Henri Nouwen, *The Wounded Healer,* henrinouwen.org, July 8

Chapter 11

1. *The Spirit Filled Bible*, NKJV, Nashville, TN, Thomas Nelson Publishers, 1991, (see chapter 4 for details), page 2025

2. Leslie Keegel, *The Spirit of the Lord is Upon Us,* Anaheim, CA, Foursquare Missions Press, 2017, pages 15-18

3. Mike Bickle, mikebickle.org, *Growing in the Prophetic*, 2010

4. Paul Hiebert, *The Excluded Middle,* hiebertglobalcenter.org.blog 2013/09

5. Winnie Long, *Miracles Unaware*, Anaheim, CA, Foursquare Missions Press, 2011

Chapter 12

1. Dan Sneed, *The Parable of the Rosebush*, Anaheim, CA, Foursquare Missions Press, 2018, pages 43-46

2. C. Peter Wagner, *Your Spiritual Gifts* (adapted), Ventura, CA, Regal Books, 1995, page 79

3. Dr. Steve Schell, *Learning to Prophesy* (sermon), 1 Corinthians 14:1-6, November 17, 2018

4. Benjamin Dixon, *Prophecy Releasing God's Voice*, Lynnwood, WA, Ignite Global Media, 2019, page 28

5. Jerry Cook and Stanley C. Baldwin, *Love, Acceptance and Forgiveness: Being Christian in a Non-Christian World*, Minneapolis, MN, Bethany House Publishers, 1979, 2009, page 32

6. Wayne Grudem, *Why Christians Can Still Prophesy,* www.waynegrudem.com, 2012/04

7. Mike Bickle, *Growing in the Prophetic,* mikebickle.org, 2010

8. Dr. Steve Schell, *Learning to Prophesy* (sermon), 1 Corinthians 14:1-6, November 17, 2018

9. David Pytches, *Spiritual Gifts in the Local Church* (adapted), Minneapolis, MN, Bethany House, 1985, page 81

10. Benjamin Dixon, *Prophecy Releasing God's Voice*, Lynnwood, WA, Ignite Global Media, 2019, page xiv

11. Teaching from good friend Rev. Cheyne Jackson

Chapter 13

1. *The Spirit Filled Bible*, NKJV, Nashville, TN, Thomas Nelson Publishers, 1991, page 1737

2. Jack Hayford Ministries/Access Digital Library, *Sorting Out Spiritual Language,* 2008

3. Jack Hayford Ministries/Access Digital Library, *Sorting Out Spiritual Language,* 2008

4. *The Spirit Filled Bible,* NKJV, Nashville, TN, Thomas Nelson Publishers, 1991

5. Sam Storm, *10 Things to Know About Speaking in Tongues*, samstorm.com, February 21, 2018

6. Sam Storm, *10 Things to Know About Speaking in Tongues*, samstorm.com, February 21, 2018

7. Randy Clark and Mary Healy, *The Spiritual Gifts Handbook*, Minneapolis, MN, Chosen Books, 2018, page 186

8. Randy Clark and Mary Healy, *The Spiritual Gifts Handbook*, Minneapolis, MN, Chosen Books, 2018, page 186

9. Randy Clark and Mary Healy, *The Spiritual Gifts Handbook*, Minneapolis, MN, Chosen Books, 2018, page 186

10. Randy Clark and Mary Healy, *The Spiritual Gifts Handbook*, Minneapolis, MN, Chosen Books, 2018, page 186

11. Randy Clark and Mary Healy, *The Spiritual Gifts Handbook*, Minneapolis, MN, Chosen Books, 2018, page 190

12. Dr. Steve Schell, *Ministering the Gift of Tongues* (sermon), July 21, 2018

Chapter 14

1. GodTube, *20 Christian End Times Quotes*, January 17, 2013

2. Bob Goff, Twitter@BobGoff, December 30, 2018

Chapter 15

1. Kenneth C. Ulmer and James O. Davis, *The Forgotten Baptism*, Oviedo, Florida, Billion Soul Publishing, 2017, page 23

2. Kenneth C. Ulmer and James O. Davis, *The Forgotten Baptism*, Oviedo, Florida, Billion Soul Publishing, 2017, page 23

3. Steve Mickel, *Walking in the Dark*, Independently published, 2019, page 503 of 1508 (Amazon/Kindle)

4. Steve Mickel, *Walking in the Dark*, Independently published, 2019, page 709 of 1508 (Amazon/Kindle)

5. Steve Mickel, *Walking in the Dark*, Independently published, 2019, page 1352 of 1508 (Amazon/Kindle)

6. Pentecostalism in Europe: A Sketch of the Dynamics, Richard Burgess, PhD, University of Birmingham, Kim Knibbe, PhD, Groningen, Netherlands, www.academia.edu

7. Pentecostalism in Europe: A Sketch of the Dynamics, Richard Burgess, PhD, University of Birmingham, Kim Knibbe, PhD, Groningen, Netherlands, www.academia.edu

8. Facebook post June 9, 2019, 4:28 pm, Surekha Hulugalle

9. Facebook post, June 16, 2019, Tom Wymore

About Foursquare Missions Press

Foursquare Missions Press (FMP) is a faith-based ministry dedicated to providing free gospel resources to developing nations.

Since 1981, FMP has partnered with 116 nations to create, print, and distribute over 220 million Bibles, books, booklets, and tracts. FMP also partners with dozens of other missional organizations to supply vitally needed gospel resources in print, digital, and video formats.

A ministry of FMP, The Children's Gospel Box has reached over a million children from 55 nations since 2002. The CG Box has trained over 20,000 children's ministry leaders, giving each one a literal box or bag filled with teaching visuals, curriculum, and literature needed for outreach and discipleship. You can learn more at **www.foursquaremissionspress.org**.

About the Authors

Dr. Jerry and Rev. Julie Stott serve as Area Missionaries to the South Pacific Region of Foursquare Churches. During their years of service they have experienced massive growth and revival in the region that now includes 18 nations and nearly 26,000 churches. Jerry and Julie currently reside in Australia with their two children and five grandchildren.

Jerry teaches all over the world on the practical approach to operating in the gifts of the Holy Spirit and is available as his schedule permits. You can contact Jerry at: **southpacific1@newmail.email**

Bob Hunt is the Director of Foursquare Missions Press. He is an author, artist, and speaker. Bob graduated from Talbot Theological Seminary (BIOLA) with an M.Div. in Intercultural Studies. He is a former missions/outreach pastor, creating non-profit organizations that served the needs of people both locally and globally. He is married to the love of his life, Heidi, a practicing attorney, residing in Southern California. You can

reach Bob directly at **bhunt@foursquare.org**.